MW00559177

EARLY CHILDHOOD E

SHARON RYAN, EDITOR

Reshaping Universal Preschool:
Critical Perspectives on Power and Policy
LUCINDA GRACE HEIMER & ANN ELIZABETH RAMMINGER, WITH KATHERINE K. DELANEY, SARAH GALANTER-GUZIEWSKI, LACEY PETERS, AND KRISTIN WHYTE

Pre-K Stories: Playing with Authorship and Integrating Curriculum in Early Childhood
DANA FRANTZ BENTLEY & MARIANA SOUTO-MANNING

Ready or Not: Early Care and Education's Leadership Choices—12 Years Later, 2nd Ed.
STACIE G. GOFFIN & VALORA WASHINGTON

Teaching STEM in the Preschool Classroom:
Exploring Big Ideas with 3- to 5-Year-Olds
ALISSA A. LANGE, KIMBERLY BRENNEMAN, & HAGIT MANO

High-Quality Early Learning for a Changing World:
What Educators Need to Know and Do
BEVERLY FALK

Guiding Principles for the New Early Childhood Professional: Building on Strength and Competence
VALORA WASHINGTON & BRENDA GADSON

Leading for Change in Early Care and Education:
Cultivating Leadership from Within
ANNE L. DOUGLASS

When Pre-K Comes to School: Policy, Partnerships, and the Early Childhood Education Workforce
BETHANY WILINSKI

Young Investigators: The Project Approach in the Early Years, 3rd Ed.
JUDY HARRIS HELM & LILIAN G. KATZ

Continuity in Children's Worlds: Choices and Consequences for Early Childhood Settings
MELISSA M. JOZWIAK, BETSY J. CAHILL, & RACHEL THEILHEIMER

The Early Intervention Guidebook for Families and Professionals: Partnering for Success, 2nd Ed.
BONNIE KEILTY

STEM Learning with Young Children:
Inquiry Teaching with Ramps and Pathways
SHELLY COUNSELL ET AL.

Courageous Leadership in Early Childhood Education:
Taking a Stand for Social Justice
SUSI LONG, MARIANA SOUTO-MANNING, & VIVIAN MARIA VASQUEZ, EDS.

Teaching Kindergarten:
Learner-Centered Classrooms for the 21st Century
JULIE DIAMOND, BETSY GROB, & FRETTA REITZES, EDS.

Healthy Learners: A Whole Child Approach to Reducing Disparities in Early Education
ROBERT CROSNOE, CLAUDE BONAZZO, & NINA WU

The New Early Childhood Professional:
A Step-by-Step Guide to Overcoming Goliath
VALORA WASHINGTON, BRENDA GADSON, & KATHRYN L. AMEL

Eight Essential Techniques for Teaching with Intention: What Makes Reggio and Other Inspired Approaches Effective
ANN LEWIN-BENHAM

Teaching and Learning in a Diverse World, 4th Ed.
PATRICIA G. RAMSEY

In the Spirit of the Studio: Learning from the *Atelier* of Reggio Emilia, 2nd Ed.
LELLA GANDINI ET AL., EDS.

Leading Anti-Bias Early Childhood Programs:
A Guide for Change
LOUISE DERMAN-SPARKS, DEBBIE LEEKEENAN, & JOHN NIMMO

Exploring Mathematics Through Play in the Early Childhood Classroom
AMY NOELLE PARKS

Becoming Young Thinkers:
Deep Project Work in the Classroom
JUDY HARRIS HELM

The Early Years Matter: Education, Care, and the Well-Being of Children, Birth to 8
MARILOU HYSON & HEATHER BIGGAR TOMLINSON

Thinking Critically About Environments for Young Children: Bridging Theory and Practice
LISA P. KUH, ED.

Standing Up for Something Every Day:
Ethics and Justice in Early Childhood Classrooms
BEATRICE S. FENNIMORE

FirstSchool: Transforming PreK–3rd Grade for African American, Latino, and Low-Income Children
SHARON RITCHIE & LAURA GUTMANN, EDS.

The States of Child Care: Building a Better System
SARA GABLE

To look for other titles in this series, visit www.tcpress.com

continued

Early Childhood Education for a New Era:
Leading for Our Profession
STACIE G. GOFFIN

Everyday Artists: Inquiry and Creativity in the Early
Childhood Classroom
DANA FRANTZ BENTLEY

Multicultural Teaching in the Early Childhood
Classroom
MARIANA SOUTO-MANNING

Inclusion in the Early Childhood Classroom
SUSAN L. RECCHIA & YOON-JOO LEE

Language Building Blocks
ANITA PANDEY

Understanding the Language Development and Early
Education of Hispanic Children
EUGENE E. GARCÍA & ERMINDA H. GARCÍA

Moral Classrooms, Moral Children, 2nd Ed.
RHETA DEVRIES & BETTY ZAN

Defending Childhood
BEVERLY FALK, ED.

Don't Leave the Story in the Book
MARY HYNES-BERRY

Starting with Their Strengths
DEBORAH C. LICKEY & DENISE J. POWERS

The Play's the Thing
ELIZABETH JONES & GRETCHEN REYNOLDS

Twelve Best Practices for Early Childhood Education
ANN LEWIN-BENHAM

Big Science for Growing Minds
JACQUELINE GRENNON BROOKS

What If All the Kids Are White? 2nd Ed.
LOUISE DERMAN-SPARKS & PATRICIA G. RAMSEY

Seen and Heard
ELLEN LYNN HALL & JENNIFER KOFKIN RUDKIN

Supporting Boys' Learning
BARBARA SPRUNG, MERLE FROSCHL, & NANCY GROPPER

Young English Language Learners
EUGENE E. GARCÍA & ELLEN C. FREDE, EDS.

Connecting Emergent Curriculum and Standards in
the Early Childhood Classroom
SYDNEY L. SCHWARTZ & SHERRY M. COPELAND

Infants and Toddlers at Work
ANN LEWIN-BENHAM

The View from the Little Chair in the Corner
CINDY RZASA BESS

Culture and Child Development in Early Childhood
Programs
CAROLLEE HOWES

Educating and Caring for Very Young Children, 2nd Ed.
DORIS BERGEN, REBECCA REID, & LOUIS TORELLI

Beginning School
RICHARD M. CLIFFORD & GISELE M. CRAWFORD, EDS.

Emergent Curriculum in the Primary Classroom
CAROL ANNE WIEN, ED.

Enthusiastic and Engaged Learners
MARILOU HYSON

Powerful Children
ANN LEWIN-BENHAM

The Early Care and Education Teaching Workforce
at the Fulcrum
SHARON LYNN KAGAN, KRISTIE KAUERZ, & KATE TARRANT

Windows on Learning, 2nd Ed.
JUDY HARRIS HELM, SALLEE BENEKE, & KATHY STEINHEIMER

Supervision in Early Childhood Education, 3rd Ed.
JOSEPH J. CARUSO WITH M. TEMPLE FAWCETT

Guiding Children's Behavior
EILEEN S. FLICKER & JANET ANDRON HOFFMAN

The War Play Dilemma, 2nd Ed.
DIANE E. LEVIN & NANCY CARLSSON-PAIGE

Possible Schools
ANN LEWIN-BENHAM

Everyday Goodbyes
NANCY BALABAN

Playing to Get Smart
ELIZABETH JONES & RENATTA M. COOPER

The Emotional Development of Young Children, 2nd Ed.
MARILOU HYSON

Young Children Continue to Reinvent Arithmetic—
2nd Grade, 2nd Ed.
CONSTANCE KAMII

Bringing Learning to Life
LOUISE BOYD CADWELL

The Colors of Learning
ROSEMARY ALTHOUSE, MARGARET H. JOHNSON,
& SHARON T. MITCHELL

A Matter of Trust
CAROLLEE HOWES & SHARON RITCHIE

Embracing Identities in Early Childhood Education
SUSAN GRIESHABER & GAILE S. CANNELLA, EDS.

Bambini: The Italian Approach to Infant/Toddler Care
LELLA GANDINI & CAROLYN POPE EDWARDS, EDS.

Serious Players in the Primary Classroom, 2nd Ed.
SELMA WASSERMANN

Young Children Reinvent Arithmetic, 2nd Ed.
CONSTANCE KAMII

Bringing Reggio Emilia Home
LOUISE BOYD CADWELL

RESHAPING UNIVERSAL PRESCHOOL

CRITICAL PERSPECTIVES ON POWER AND POLICY

Lucinda G. Heimer
Ann Elizabeth Ramminger

WITH CONTRIBUTIONS BY

Katherine K. Delaney, Sarah Galanter-Guziewski,
Lacey Peters, and Kristin Whyte

Foreword by M. Elizabeth Graue

TEACHERS COLLEGE PRESS

TEACHERS COLLEGE | COLUMBIA UNIVERSITY

NEW YORK AND LONDON

Published by Teachers College Press®, 1234 Amsterdam Avenue, New York, NY 10027

Cover photo by HQuality / Shutterstock.

Chapter 3 is adapted from Lucinda Heimer's "Voices at the Table: The Deconstruction of the Policy Process for a Local Preschool Initiative." In Sharon Ryan and Susan Grieshaber (Eds), *Practical Transformations and Transformational Practices: Globalization, Postmodernism, and Early Childhood Education*. New York, NY: Elsevier. © 2006 Lucinda Heimer.

Appendix is adapted from Lucinda Heimer's "Power, power who's got the power? Understanding collaboration in the implementation of a public kindergarten for 4-year-olds" (Doctoral dissertation). Ann Arbor, MI: UMI Dissertation Services (No. 288).

Photography by Lucinda Heimer. Images titled: Everyone Counts, Play, Together, Entering New Territory, Whose Turf, Engaged in Learning, Kids' Interests, I See You, Patience, and Interlocking.

Library of Congress Cataloging-in-Publication Data

Names: Heimer, Lucinda Grace, author. | Ramminger, Elizabeth Ann, author.
Title: Reshaping universal preschool : critical perspectives on power and policy / Lucinda Grace Heimer, Elizabeth Ann Ramminger ; with contributions by Katherine K. Delaney, Sarah Galanter-Guziewski, Lacey Peters, and Kristin Whyte ; foreword by Elizabeth Graue.
Description: New York, NY : Teachers College Press, 2020. | Includes bibliographical references and index. |
Identifiers: LCCN 2019039267 | ISBN 9780807761267 (paperback) | ISBN 9780807761274 (hardcover) | ISBN 9780807778128 (ebook)
Subjects: LCSH: Education, Preschool--United States. | Education, Preschool--Government policy--United States. | Education and state--United States.
Classification: LCC LB1140.23 .H435 2020 | DDC 372.21--dc23
LC record available at https://lccn.loc.gov/2019039267

ISBN 978-0-8077-6126-7 (paper)
ISBN 978-0-8077-6127-4 (hardcover)
ISBN 978-0-8077-7812-8 (ebook)

Printed on acid-free paper
Manufactured in the United States of America

In memory of my father,
Roger Lee Heimer,
my first beloved teacher

Contents

Foreword

In today's early education context, where discussions about public pre-K programs seem to be everywhere, it can be challenging to remember a time when the idea of allocating public funding for programs for children younger than kindergarten was just plain crazy talk. Political candidates, the media, and researchers, among others, bandy it about, framed variously as an economic issue, an equity flashpoint, as something for "other families," or a contested research knowledge base. Wait, don't we already have public pre-K?

No, not yet. We have Head Start and Early Childhood Special Education, both federally funded programs for specific subgroups of children that do not serve all eligible children. If we consider those programs and state-funded programs, we can only account for 44% of 4-year-olds and 16% of 3-year-olds, and many are not full day (Friedman-Krauss, Barnett, et al., 2019). It's important that we also recognize that we are not past the "Should the public pay for early education programs?" question when we consider the state of kindergarten. Only 13 states plus the District of Columbia require full-day kindergarten (which is full only in relation to the school day), with 35 states reporting that 70–89% of students attend full day (Atchison, Parker, & Diffey, 2016).

This chaotic early education landscape is part of a very messy policy ecology marked by considerations that are at the heart of Heimer and Ramminger's volume, *Reshaping Universal Preschool: Critical Perspectives on Power and Policy*. In this multivocal, time-traveling, theory-spiced reading of a pilot pre-K program and later districtwide implementation, the authors engage us in a portrayal of the complexity of what amounts to major social change[1]. Rather than simply adding services to the public school programming, public pre-K cannot avoid stirring up a hornet's nest of conflicting needs, values, goals, and resources. And because participants are not equally positioned, what should be an equity-promoting addition often seems to recreate systems of winners and losers. The good intentions that motivated the actors in Heimer, Ramminger, and their colleagues' recounting of public pre-K implementation—and I know that there were very good intentions—were frequently tangled up in the fault lines among different agencies.

---

1. Peters's essay of New York City's high-profile public pre-K program does not deal with the focal district's implementation but adds to our understanding by bringing our attention to important issues in the current context.

The many perspectives presented in this book are appropriately cacopho-nous—words of policy scholars, theorists, researchers, teachers, parents, admin-istrators, and even children are not congruous or in harmony. That is because public pre-K touches many lives. It involves many agencies, and it has many goals. Books like *Reshaping Universal Preschool: Critical Perspectives on Power and Policy* are a reminder that we are probably in the midst of figuring out a sticky policy problem that does not have a solution, yet. It is a work in progress, a work that we all have a stake in.

—M. Elizabeth Graue, Sorenson Professor of Curriculum and Instruction, School of Education at the University of Wisconsin–Madison

REFERENCES

Atchison, B., Parker, E., & Diffey, L. (2016). *Full-day kindergarten: A look across the states.* Denver, CO: Education Commission of the States.

Friedman-Krauss, A. H., Barnett, W. S., Garver, K. A., Hodges, K. S., Weisenfeld, G. G., & DiCrecchio, N. (2019). *The state of preschool 2018: State preschool yearbook.* New Brunswick, NJ: National Institute for Early Education Research.

Acknowledgments

When we speak about how much early childhood matters, it comes deep from our own hearts and souls. Both of us have fond memories of our earliest years and extend gratitude to our families of origin for all they offered. All children deserve great beginnings.

Heartfelt appreciation goes out to our families for their patience as we balanced this work with spending time with them. A special dedication goes out to family members whom we lost during the writing of this book.

Many professional experiences have shaped who we are as authors. We would like to thank the mentors, colleagues, researchers, practitioners, and families who have inspired us to explore and write about our passion.

We have respect and gratitude for the contributing authors. With great faith, little lead time, and amazing graciousness, Katherine K. Delaney, Sarah Galanter-Guziewski, Lacey Peters, and Kristin Whyte offered critical insights in the "Present" stories. It was a gift to see our work together unfold as the stories seamlessly lined up to bolster our insights and recommendations.

We express our appreciation to the reviewers and editorial staff at TC Press, especially Sarah Biondello, Jennifer Baker, and series editor Sharon Ryan, who helped make this book happen. We thank Beth Graue for her wisdom and advocacy in early childhood education. Providing support and input for the research, the spark of the idea for the book, and writing the Foreword were much appreciated gifts.

Lucy: I am impressed by the dedication and creativity of educators, most especially those in this book, working hard to create nurturing experiences and environments for all children. They are the champions of the cause and our efforts to represent these stories are in earnest to celebrate effort and craft change.

Writing this book was my most challenging endeavor to date. It was a labor of love and, therefore, riddled with angst and trepidation for honoring the voices, real and created. We are always learning. Completing this project was only possible with the help of my support network. I am honored to work with amazing colleagues, friends, and editors. I am humbled by the patience and creative spirit of my collaborator Ann. Drs. Beth Graue, Gloria Ladson-Billings, and Mimi Bloch expertly served as mentors at the inception of this research and throughout my career. I am grateful to the children, families, educators, administrators, researchers, and staff who made the original research possible. They shared their experiences and stories with grace and dedication. Colleagues and students both in Boston and at UW–Whitewater have inspired me and brought depth to my understanding of curious inquiry. Many thanks to Robin Fox for her compassionate decisiveness and the entire UWW ECE team: You model care, creativity, and commitment.

We teach from our lived experiences, who we are. I am indebted to my family, biological and chosen. When my father died earlier this year, I was reminded of his commitment to social justice, to end gun violence, to support racial and economic equity, and his legacy of education and ministry. My mother, an author herself, is a model of strength, compassion, and creative leadership. Words cannot express my respect for the wisdom of wonder my daughters, Grace and Amalia, share with me each day. Grace's namesake, my grandmother, taught in a one-room schoolhouse, and my aunt Arlene, now 100 and a retired early childhood educator, provide models of teaching across time. Thanks to Drew and Julia for "always in your love, standing by." My partner Chris offered support to complete this project, often requiring juggling acts. Family members named and not named are the center of my life.

Ann: As a seasoned early childhood professional who has dipped toes in many early education pools, I have strong feelings that our society can offer more to our youngest children and their families. I want to thank Lucy for inviting me to be a partner in this important work—to call for equity in early education and more meaningful connections to the K–12 system. Her passion shines through the fog of complexity. There are many others along my professional path that have shaped my passion and perceptions. I thank them all.

From a personal perspective, many thanks go out to my husband Bob whose energy and understanding kept me on a steady course. To my children who fondly remember their early childhood years camping, backpacking, and living in the country. And to my family of origin who kept my early childhood years joyful through very difficult times. Kudos to my nieces, who are engaged in important work with young children and their families.

Preface

"Wisdom begins in wonder." —Socrates

As we embark on the journey to share our passion, we must honor the complexity of finding a space for action when so many seemingly opposing factors are at work. It is helpful to reflect on the impetus for this book—children. Our youngest children lead the way in how the future will be crafted, hopefully with ways of knowing that are open, curious, and full of wonder.

There is power in the wisdom of wonder. How will we honor that wisdom as we design systems to support all children and families? In this book, we join the synergy of wonder to the practicality of wisdom to navigate complicated systems of power, relationships, and discourse.

Universal Preschool is a frequent issue in the political landscape as having potential to address the woes of the formal education system and give children their best start on their educational path as well as their lives. We hope investment and creativity in early childhood education will remain an important topic of discussion. This book is timely as questions regarding access, equity, and the societal value of early childhood education enter into the public forum for political discussion (Bouffard, 2017; Interlandi, 2018).

TERMINOLOGY

The terminology for Universal Preschool varies and has changed over time. We use the term *Universal Preschool* to identify programs designed for and offered at no cost to all 3- and 4-year-old children. Other terms frequently used include *UPK*, *Universal Prekindergarten*, *Universal Pre-K*, *Public Pre-K*, *3K*, and *4K*. Both the terms *Universal Preschool* and *UPK* are gaining national attention on the political and social fronts, and are easily recognized in the field of early childhood education (ECE). We implore the reader to consider the danger in referring to all early years as Pre-K or 4K, as this prioritizes the connection with formal K–12 education systems. Even the term *UPK* has loaded meaning because in this acronym kindergarten is named while the earlier years are ill-defined. We argue that preschool deserves to be treated as unique, not conflated with kindergarten. For example, if Universal Preschool is interpreted as only 4K, and enrolls only 4-year-olds, the universal access to preschool basically becomes defined as "kindergarten for 4-year-olds." It is no longer prekindergarten; instead, it essentially becomes the "new kindergarten." This begs consideration of how, as a nation, we define and label early education as a unique, but related, system of support for children and families from birth onward.

Although the term *Universal Preschool* suggests that enrollment is open to all children, the capacity and criteria vary by state and do not guarantee enrollment (Barnett & Gomez, 2016). In addition, a variety of regulations, standards, and requirements exist to oversee the diverse early education services provided by Head Start, child care, and public schools. The need to communicate across the various institutions, organizations, and agencies brings up issues of power structures, curricular philosophies, and funding sources. These issues remain a constant factor for Universal Preschool across time.

Similar terminology issues arise when labeling early education. There are many terms that are used, including *early childhood education, early education and care, early care and education, child care*, and *day care*. We will use the terms *early education* and *early childhood education* interchangeably throughout the text.

We have included Terminology Tips to clarify certain concepts, definitions, and academic terms. These tips on terminology are offered to aid the reader in accessing and applying critical ideas.

A DILEMMA

Conversations around early education and Universal Preschool compete with many other pressing social issues. Who has the power to speak for all young children and families? Who is taking the time to do so? There is a need to discuss, promote, and address the issue of equity in early education. Those who are passionate about young children and their families understand the need to bring this issue to the forefront. What can bring wonder to these needed discussions and wisdom to our actions?

OUR LENS

The issue of Universal Preschool is not new. Others have conducted research and shared success stories and ideas for moving forward. We plan a different approach to the Universal Preschool dilemma by using the following lens to sift through the layers of power and policy that are the foundation of any effort. Using this approach we provide next steps in offering equitable and relevant early education for preschool children.

Past/Present Stories

Chapters 3, 4, and 5 feature UPK collaboration stories that focus on the interplay of power and discourse in participation, access, curricula, and leadership. These "Past" and "Present" stories span 15 years of Universal Preschool policy implementation to bring alive the complexity of collaboration. All data for the "Past" stories were gathered between 2001 and 2004. "Present" stories are from Universal Preschool initiatives and research in the past 5 years.

Critical Theory

"'Critical Theory' refers to a specific scholarly approach that explores the historical, cultural and ideological lines of authority that underlie social conditions" (Sensoy & DiAngelo, 2017, p. 1). Using critical theory, we acknowledge the inherent complications of addressing Universal Preschool in the context of the broader ECE system. Specifically, we examine the needs of a pluralistic society that span the public and private sectors.

Power

We highlight the power (individual/systemic/political) relationships that circulate in early childhood education contexts. Such power relationships are illuminated in the "Past" and "Present" stories presented throughout this book. We acknowledge both the changing nature (Foucault, 1980) and the relational impact of power (Bourdieu, 1977).

Discourse

Discourses constructed through power relationships provide one way of explaining phenomena that shape our perceptions of an event or topic. The discourses of collaboration and universal access are explored in "Past" and "Present" stories from UPK initiatives.

Reflective Conversations and Actions

Each chapter contains reflective questions to highlight key concepts in this book and complexities around Universal Preschool. We encourage readers to keep an open and curious mind while engaging in these conversations.

> When we are trying to figure out something perplexing (for which we often use the term "a problem"), or when we are facing uncertainty (for which we use the term "change"), it seems natural to our western way of thinking to quickly find the right answer to some questions: "Exactly what is the cause of this? What's going on

here? How are things going to unfold? What is likely to happen? What should be our plan?" (J. Brown, 2007, p. 107, as described to her by Paula Underwood)

Coming up with a solution to a problem too soon, and without thoughtfully conversing with others of varying perspectives, stifles curiosity and imaginative thinking. Keeping open to a sense of wonder, to possibilities, inspires creative thinking and ultimately honors many perspectives in final decisions and actions. Before we jump to "the plan," it may be wise to slow down and ponder the multifaceted complexities of a collaborative effort.

We offer the following insight for creative and open thought. The Rule of Six, a thinking process originating with the Oneida peoples of the Iroquois Confederacy, requires looking at a situation from at least six different perspectives before deciding on an action (Underwood, 1993). This thinking process accomplishes several things: It keeps our perceptions open to a broader range of data; it helps in "systems thinking"; and it creates flexibility in our thinking. Linear cause-and-effect approaches are viewed as efficient in policy work, but too often limit the possibility for change. Engaging in a more reflective thinking process allows us to honor many perspectives as we approach collaborative efforts.

Perspectives

> The reading of another's story is always a partial telling, bound not only by one's perspective but also by the exigencies of what can and cannot be told. The narratives of lived experiences—the story, or what is told, and the discourse, or what it is that structures how a story is told—are always selective, partial, and in tension. (Britzman, 1991, p. 13)

The retelling of the "Past" and "Present" stories is bound by perspective; and these stories are influenced by and structured through discourse. We know what we know based only on our experiences and circumstances. We cannot help but see things from our own point of view (Sensoy & DiAngelo, 2017)—a seemingly simple idea, and yet crucial to explore as we create early education policy that honors the diverse lives of our youngest community members. It takes real work to listen and understand someone else's perspective on any given topic or situation. Given that we acknowledge the importance of power as relational (Bourdieu, 1977), it makes sense to consider how key players in the Universal Preschool movement enact and embody policy in collaborative efforts. Universal Preschool collaborations are unique because they involve stakeholders with varying levels of education, experiences, cultures, socioeconomic backgrounds, and knowledge of early childhood education. While we acknowledge that it is not possible to provide a voice and perspective for all individuals and groups, we attempt to share how others might perceive an issue or situation.

We explore perspectives in three ways throughout the book:

1. Through the use of data, we share stories of a past UPK collaboration; quotes and data from research presented in Past stories are referenced/cited in parenthetical notes following the data.[1]
2. We offer examples of present Universal Preschool initiatives.
3. We provide perspective through the voices of those who may be interested or involved in Universal Preschool collaboratives. Vignettes and text boxes are amalgams of voices from the community.

Families: Children do not live in isolation. They are part of families and communities bringing myriad traditions, languages, and experience to the process. How do we honor a spirit of partnership to help a family's child grow and learn? How and when is the family's voice heard and respected?

Teachers: Teachers are the heart of the program and yet they often are left without the tools or information they need to do their job. How do these teachers straddle the early childhood and elementary education worlds? How do they work at the intersection of written and enacted (curriculum) policy? How do they equitably meet the needs of all children?

Related and Support Staff: What about support staff—do these individuals feel valued? Every interaction with a young child counts, including classroom assistants, special education providers, bus drivers, food service staff, and so on.

Educational Administrators: How can educational leaders set the stage for successful programs? They are tasked with supporting staff to gain the necessary knowledge, skills, and dispositions, yet are also accountable to budget constraints. How do they assist teachers to set up engaging classrooms and promote effective instruction to enhance child outcomes? How do they negotiate bureaucratic pressures and meet the unique needs of staff, families, and constituents?

Policymakers/Researchers: How do policymakers understand the value of funding high-quality early childhood education? How is UPK viewed at the federal, state, and local levels? What is needed to support the required changes toward equity in ECE?

General Public: How is ECE viewed as a public right or responsibility? How does the lack of public understanding about the importance of the early childhood years play a role? How do we inform the public and how might we attract more professionals to the field of early childhood education?

---

1. Pseudonyms are used throughout the text for people, places, and organizations. First names are used to facilitate readability.

CHAPTER SUMMARIES

Chapter 1, "Early Education in the United States: Is It Fair Game?" begins the discussion of how ECE fits into the larger educational and societal context, and why we should care. Given the mosaic of ECE policies, programs, funding, and governance, opening Universal Preschool to all young children as a public option requires strong collaborative approaches. This is not always an easy task due to a variety of regulations, standards, and requirements that have evolved to oversee the diverse early education services provided in the United States on the national, regional, and local levels (Zigler, Gilliam, & Jones, 2006).

Chapter 2, "Universal Preschool: Panacea or Perpetuated Patchwork," focuses on Universal Preschool history, trends, and complexities. It outlines how Universal Preschool is affected by the various funding sources and requirements of early childhood systems, such as federal (e.g., Head Start), private (e.g., child care), and local (e.g., public schools) (Zigler, Gilliam, & Jones, 2006). These diverse influences require collaboration across sectors. We explore the notion of collaboration and define and illustrate how power and discourse influence collaboration and leadership of Universal Preschool initiatives (Foucault, 1980). It is in this chapter that we introduce the case study that provides data for the Past stories.

Chapter 3, "Encouraging All Voices in the Universal Preschool Conversation," provides insight on building social capital and alliances, and crafting counternarratives to those steeped in either privilege or oppression. This chapter explores these power dynamics with consideration of various forms of capital (Bourdieu, 1977), using examples of community and classroom meetings held to implement and roll out Universal Preschool initiatives. During the planning or implementation stage of Universal Preschool, many issues arise around funding, enrollment, staff, curriculum, child assessment, family engagement, and transportation. Positional and organizational power differentials may create obstacles during this time, when stakeholders are trying to find mutual agreement. Some voices will dominate while other individuals/groups may feel disempowered.

Chapter 4, "Equitable Access to Universal Preschool," explores early childhood enrollment policy as it impacts both school district and Head Start sites. The often-conflicting agendas of diverse agencies are viewed through the lens of critical race theory (CRT), specifically interest convergence (Bell, 1987). We explore how enrollment policy creates illogical consequences that test the idea that enrollment is truly universal for all children and families. Issues including the confusing nature of federal, state, and local policy; turf; and location all play into enrollment decisions. Checking in with key stakeholders throughout the process is required.

Chapter 5, "Leading the Curriculum Process," covers the complicated nature of collaboration required in Universal Preschool movements. It explores

barriers and strengths of collaborative leadership in the process of implementing curriculum in early childhood classrooms. As teachers implement the
curriculum, questions regarding curriculum choice and leadership are raised.
This multifaceted form of leadership, frustrating and cumbersome, creates the
possibility for autonomy and relational leadership (Burch & Spillane, 2004;
Douglass, 2017; Good, 2018).

Chapter 6, "A Long and Winding Road," recaps the insights offered
throughout the book. Universal Preschool offers an opportunity to address
issues of equity in the United States, with recognition of power, assumptions,
and discourses at play. Insights include (1) collaborative efforts are required in
Universal Preschool, as this work is inherently cross-sector; (2) the term UPK
(Universal Prekindergarten) is problematic as it subsumes early education
(birth to age 5) into the K–12 system. Therefore, we suggest *Universal Preschool*
as a more accurate term; and (3) Universal Preschool offers an opportunity
to address issues of equity in the United States, with recognition of power,
assumptions, and discourses at play.

OUR HOPES

Given the diverse auspices and leadership in early education in the United
States, Universal Preschool will happen only through collaboration. Given
that equity in power is not static, collaboration is elusive. One goal of this
book is to take into consideration larger discourses as well as individual interpretations of the process. Therefore, it takes work to address assumptions
as issues of power imbalances and differentials emerge, defined by culture,
language, race, and ability, among other factors. So, what makes this collaborative policy work worth doing? The United States is in crisis in education, looking to standardize and assess based on uniform/universal notions.
Through early education solutions we can avoid the pitfalls of our existing,
yet archaic, formal education systems; instead, we can explore creative solutions that honor the wisdom in wonder.

We hope readers will find this book helpful in whatever path of life they
are traveling today, as well as where they may venture in the future. Throughout our careers, we have noticed upticks in interest in early childhood education when citizens are faced with immediate needs in their own families,
either through emergent necessity or careful planning. We suggest that sustained interest and support for children and their families, and the communities in which they live, are in the best interests of all citizens. Let's keep the
conversation alive!

Judy Brown (2007) nicely sums up the need for all voices to contribute to
this conversation in her poem:

Everybody Counts

Everybody counts.
When the spider
Weaves the web
No connecting point
Is missed.
If you are missing
From our midst
We are the lesser
For that loss,
And incomplete.

CHAPTER 1

Early Education in the United States
Is It Fair Game?

"There can be no keener revelation of a society's soul than the way in which it treats its children."

—Nelson Mandela, former president of South Africa

Think of that magical moment when you discover something for the first time. Reflect on the adrenaline rush, the joy that emanates from your being, the confidence you feel as you share your new discovery with another. How do we define that moment with and for our children? How do we translate wonder and discovery as learning and development? How is the learning and development of young children understood, valued, and funded? As a democratic nation, with economic means, why are we behind other countries in providing comprehensive supports and services for young children and their families? These powerful questions guide the exploration of how policy and discourse at all levels affect families with young children and the journey for educational equity.

In this chapter, we explore how decisions are made in the United States to fund formal schooling, highlight how early education fits into our nation's political debates, and consider ways faculty, leaders, and teachers in early education demographically represent (or do not represent) the population of students, families, and communities.

For decades, we have known that brain development in the early years impacts future development (Center on the Developing Child, 2011; Shonkoff & Phillips, 2000). This text moves beyond this argument to offer history, context, and stories to frame next steps for creatively providing early education in the United States for all young children.

TERMINOLOGY TIPS

Early childhood education (ECE) and *early education* will be used interchangeably as a general term for the profession. Other terms often used include *early care and education, early education and care, preschool, child care,* and *day care.*

Across the globe, each society decides what is best for its citizens, including families and their youngest children. The social construct of what childhood means, has changed over time and varies internationally (Cannella & Viruru, 2004; Mayall, 2002; Rogoff, 2003; Wells, 2015; Wollons, 2000). Failing to honor the complexity of childhood has led, at times, to misguided efforts (or lack of effort) in the best interests of families with young children. At the most sensitive time, young children and their families may not be provided with the types of services and resources that promote their health, safety, and educational needs. The societal construct of childhood impacts how funding is allocated, policies are crafted and implemented, and public attitudes are shaped toward young children and their families. These social constructs form the basis for educational equity and shape the general direction of public policy.

TERMINOLOGY TIPS

We use the term *equitable access* to describe the need to offer varying levels of support to achieve a greater fairness of outcomes for all children and families. This goes beyond *equal access*, which typically signifies providing the same levels of support for all segments of society.

It is assumed that everyone will benefit from the same supports. They are being treated equally.	Individuals are given different supports to make it possible for them to have equal access to the game. They are being treated equitably.	All three can see the game without any supports or accommodations because the cause of the inequity was addressed. The systemic barrier has been removed.

Graphic courtesy of Advancing Equity and Inclusion: A Guide for Municipalities, by City for All Women Initiative (CAWI), Ottawa, Canada.

How many children actually attend some kind of preschool? According to Barnett, Weisenfeld, Brown, Squires, and Horowitz (2016), somewhat less than 70% of 4-year-olds are regularly enrolled in some kind of preschool. Even fewer 3-year-olds attend preschool—a tad over 40%. Children who most need early education may not be enrolled in preschool, even though Head Start and state preschool programs target children living in poverty or with high needs. In fact, children in families with lower income are less likely to be in center-based early education programs and more likely to be in relative care (Capizzano & Adams, 2004).

The preference for relative care may be due to many factors, but one common factor is the high cost of child care. The percentages noted above suggest the need for programs that simply "provide care" for working families, yet this is only one goal in early childhood policy and program creation. The large number of families who need and enroll in ECE supports further exploration of alternatives to the national, state, and local early childhood education and care systems.

TERMINOLOGY TIPS

Relative care refers to the child's family or extended family, whereas *family child care* refers to child-care providers who provide "fee for services" care in their homes.

Universal Preschool often is seen as a fix to the early childhood equation, without considering the broader picture of the birth to age 5 system that typically falls under the auspices of human services. In fact, some voices would like to include prenatal systems to age 8 in a more comprehensive education system of support. How do we define human services and education systems, and where does one system begin and another end? Should there be one system? Why has Universal Preschool come to be the panacea to fix 3rd-grade reading scores and boost academic achievement? It is helpful to view these questions through a societal and historical lens to understand where we have been and where we might go to bring equity to young children and their families.

EDUCATIONAL EQUITY IN THE UNITED STATES—A QUICK HISTORY

There have been varying beliefs and efforts to support families and young children in the United States across time. For instance, how has society come to view early childhood education as more custodial in nature (often referred to as day care) and formal schooling (usually K–12) as a profession? How does Universal Preschool lie in the middle of this perception?

Women's Rights

Women's rights and the care and education of young children currently are inextricably intertwined. Since caring for young children is traditionally seen as a female responsibility, it has limited the ability of women to engage in professions outside of the home and family. In general, the work of rearing young children does not have a monetary value placed on it, even though it has societal value. However, insufficient family leave policies and lack of adequate funding at the national and state levels suggest a lack of value at the societal level. The Family and Medical Leave Act (FMLA) was passed in 1993, offering increased job security to address family needs, but little has changed since then (U.S. Department of Labor, 2019). The care of young children often is divided along cultural, racial, and class lines. Families with sufficient incomes can afford to have a family member stay home with their children or can pay for quality in- or out-of-home education and care. Historically, families living at or below the poverty level, who themselves needed to work outside the home, had few options for care and education of their children. Too often these few options did not offer culturally authentic and relevant care.

Infant School Movement

The infant school movement during the 1830s, which was founded on Christian principles, held a strong focus on the family and offered specialized programming (Beatty, 1995). The movements of the 1800s placed a strong emphasis on family, similar to the contemporary Christian movements under the "focus on family" banner. Following the infant school movement, the first kindergarten in America, Froebel's kindergarten, was started in Watertown, Wisconsin, in 1856.

Kindergarten Movement

The late 1800s marked the beginning of the kindergarten movement, which began to address universal public kindergartens (Beatty, 1995). The creation of the public kindergarten, nearly 150 years ago, became a battle between private and public interests and between female kindergarten teachers and male administrators and principals (Beatty, 1995). The early childhood education focus, during the period coinciding with World War I, was the importance of Americanizing the nation. A conflict appeared between the earlier child-centered philosophies and the political agenda of the early 1900s. Additional battles over pedagogy, philosophy, and control of early education emerged. At the same time, children of color gained slower access to kindergarten programs because kindergartens were not created in the South as quickly as in the North. From 1910 to 1930, private nurseries were experiencing a pedagogical movement away from the family (away from Froebel) toward a societal influence supported by Freudian philosophies. The family was still considered an important influence on the child, but childhood independence became a new pedagogical component (Beatty, 1995).

Child Care During World War II

World War II changed the societal perspective on the value of women and led to a significant piece of legislation to help working women with young children. The Lanham Act, passed during World War II, provided a limited nationwide program of child-care centers. The primary goal of these programs was to free up mothers to contribute to war production efforts and to provide jobs for unemployed teachers. This national recognition that women were important contributors to society brought about increased discussion of the care and education of young children outside of the home (Michel, 2011).

After World War II, many women were forced to give up their jobs to men returning from service. Many families needed only one wage earner, so families were able to have one parent stay home with young children. This somewhat decreased the demand for early education outside of the home (Roosevelt, 1944).

War on Poverty and Head Start

In the 1950s, Sputnik revived the national push for globally competitive citizens, and the 1960s brought Lyndon Johnson's War on Poverty and, in 1965, the compensatory Head Start program (Michel, 1999). There was a concerted effort to require that mothers living in poverty work outside the home in order to receive any kind of government benefit. Many pieces of legislation were offered and enacted, debating the merits of providing child care with a continuing patchwork approach across states and communities. As the 1960s continued, exploration of the impact of early education was highlighted through research and pilot programs such as the Perry Preschool Project (1962–1967) (Schweinhart & Weikart, 1997). These programs, targeting specific populations of children, were the first to acknowledge the pivotal role of early development. This was a significant point in history in the political and societal recognition of the importance of preschool for all children.

Universal Preschool

Although somewhat universal access to kindergarten was created at the turn of the 20th century, preschools remained segregated into different options for families. There were private partial-day and full-day programs (illustrating parents' right to choose "early education" depending on their economic means), and Head Start remained an option for families with a lower income, offering primarily partial-day programs but with some full-day options. Over the past

17 years (2002–2019), many states have created universal access to preschool, or 4-year-old kindergarten (4K), which eventually may allow access for all children, as the age at which we define kindergarten shifts to younger age groups (Friedman-Krauss et al., 2019). How we define kindergarten and preschool are of paramount importance to this discussion.

PUBLIC EDUCATION

Historical education movements in the United States provide a backdrop for understanding the current Universal Preschool movement. Abowitz (2003) provides helpful insight in terms of the history and nature of public education by describing the problematic notion that public and private spheres function separately. Pulling from Kaestle's (1983) work in reference to Horace Mann and the common school movement in the United States, Abowitz (2003) suggests:

> A mix of ideologies lent themselves as rationale for a universal public school system: a republican notion of democratic citizenship for all, accompanied by liberal conceptions of autonomy and of the welfare state as inclusive of the poor. Public schools were free for the poor and rich, and the system evolved as universal in the sense that it was designed, by and large, to serve the children of all families regardless of status or wealth. (p. 85)

While K–12 public education systems were created in the early 1900s under these auspices, research suggests "that racial segregation in some American schools remains at levels equal to or surpassing the levels in existence when the *Brown v. Board of Education* decision was handed down [in 1954]" (Orfield & Eaton, 1996, as cited in Abowitz, 2003, p. 86). More recently, as reported in a *New York Times* article, EdBuild (2019), a catalyst organization, found "that more than half of the nation's schoolchildren are in racially concentrated districts, where over 75% of students are either white or nonwhite" (Meatto, 2019). Taking a critical perspective provides some explanation for how this disconnection between perceived intent and practice occurs, and acknowledges the conflicts and struggles that exist among unequal classes and social groups (Gomez-Velez, 2015). For example, Malcom Gladwell (2017) explored whether the original intent of *Brown v. Board of Education* was understood and represented in legislature. He suggests that the lawsuit was less about a need for integration and more about equity in terms of publicly offered resources for community members to teach in their home communities. Issues of continued segregation provide the impetus to consider the current rhetoric surrounding Universal Preschool in the United States. Sweeping policy reform inherently creates dynamics of inclusion and exclusion. As we revisit historical education reform, we are able to consider next steps in relation to separate systems for young children.

WHY SHOULD EARLY EDUCATION BE TREATED DIFFERENTLY?

One goal of the public education system is to provide access to the knowledge and experiences necessary for full engagement in a democratic society (Apple, 2018). While imperfect, this movement in the United States shifted the opportunities for entire groups of citizens by providing at least the hope of access to education. Currently, the push for children to meet standards based on prescribed timelines has created an educational environment demanding academic rigor (Fuller, 2007). As Universal Preschool increasingly is defined as 4K or 3K, it is essential to analyze the impact of this pressure on the curricula designed for younger students.

> ### RESEARCHER PERSPECTIVE
>
> Early experiences affect the development of brain architecture, which provides the foundation for all future learning, behavior, and health. Just as a weak foundation compromises the quality and strength of a house, adverse experiences early in life can impair brain architecture, with negative effects lasting into adulthood.

We know more about brain architecture than we ever have before, and there are increasing data to show that the early years are critical. In the first few years of life, more than 1 million new neural connections form every second, thus making the impact of early experiences and interactions a compelling societal concern (Institute of Medicine, 2000; Thompson, 2014). In addition, child psychology and developmental theorists have long reinforced what many early childhood professionals know—young children learn through hands-on, experiential activities and purposeful play (Riley et al., 2007). The common perception of "play" as the opposite of work and not resulting in something productive can undermine understanding of the "real work of play" for young children. Through play, young children make sense of their world in practical and symbolic ways that set the stage for future learning (Frost, Wortham, & Reifel, 2012). This is an important consideration in how early childhood programs are structured and how teachers and other personnel are educated (Gary, 2010; Golinkoff, Hassinger-Das, & Hirsh-Pasek, 2017; Weisberg, Kittredge, Hirsh-Pasek, Golinkoff, & Klahr, 2015; Wohlwend & Peppler, 2015).

When one considers the unique learning styles and needs of each child (at any age), might the pedagogy used in early education be a better approach to helping all children reach their potential? When a standardized curriculum becomes the blanket approach, differentiation of learning becomes more challenging. This can lead to the push-down of kindergarten through grade 3 (K–3) educational practices into publicly funded preschools.

The history and structure of the K–12 educational system can impede the efforts of early childhood advocates to change our societal mindset. As we have

Play

learned from the efforts of Head Start and other holistic programs, focusing on academics without addressing underlying issues such as health (physical, emotional, social), nutrition, family supports, and community connections may not have the desired results (Center on the Developing Child, 2011). This also can lead to further complications for children as they age and can even have negative societal effects overall.

If we value the importance of learning in the early years, should we not also value how this learning is structured and offered? Herein lies a dilemma in providing universal access to early learning opportunities. There is a concerted emphasis on "school readiness," which has been defined by Head Start as "children are ready for school, families are ready to support their children's learning, and schools are ready for children" (Head Start Early Childhood Learning and Knowledge Center, 2019).

Perhaps we are asking the wrong questions. The question is not how do we get children ready for school, but how do we rethink what school looks like for children (Graue, 2006)? Specifically, for young children through the elementary grades in the United States, education communities flourish when they represent family home bases both culturally and linguistically. This requires a reciprocal relationship between home and school settings, a relationship in which the whole child is considered. How do we define "school" in the early years and how do we then prepare these schools to be ready for children?

THE CURRENT U.S. EARLY EDUCATION SYSTEM—A PATCHWORK

There is a patchwork of national policy and funding for the comprehensive delivery of high-quality early childhood programs and services in the United States. This is in addition to a lack of national policy guiding when children should start formal schooling. There are also wide differences among the states in how the K–12 educational system is funded and implemented. How can the case be made for Universal Preschool when only 17 states, plus the District of Columbia, require children to attend kindergarten (currently defined as kindergarten for 5-year-olds) (Diffey, 2017)? Of those 17 states, only 13 (plus the District of Columbia) require their districts to offer full-day kindergarten.

Following a different regulatory procedure than public K–12 systems, early childhood education is provided in both licensed and nonlicensed settings. Licensing is typically at the state level and includes regulation and oversight of group child-care centers, public and private preschools, family child-care homes, and school-age/after-school programs. There can be great variation in the purpose, size, and structure of these programs (e.g., corporate-sponsored, faith-based, for-profit, nonprofit, Head Start, camps, dance, environmental, etc.). Some states have regulations that allow for family and kinship care (with fewer numbers of children and/or caring for children of relatives); these programs may be licensed or registered. Some of these licensed programs enroll families who receive child-care subsidies, and other programs do not, as doing so can require additional paperwork and coordination.

Providers may not know they need to be regulated or may choose not to be regulated; this is considered unlicensed care. There are an undetermined number of individuals providing unlicensed care throughout the United States. In unlicensed settings, there is little way to measure quality of care and education for young children. Some families choose to juggle work schedules

FAMILY PERSPECTIVE

I knew I'd have to think ahead for enrolling in preschool, but I had no idea that the center down the street would be full. I searched online and heard from friends that at a minimum the center should be licensed. I'm really not sure what that means, but I do think credentials are important. I think I'd feel most at ease if Divya was in a small setting, more home-like. Should I ask at our neighborhood association meeting? Where do I go to find out where the care is focused on nurturing and teaching values we have at home?

to avoid enrolling their children in early education programs with additional costs. Families also may share child-care responsibilities with relatives, friends, or neighbors. This may work well for families; however, it is another piece to consider in the complex early education system puzzle. As broad policies are passed, this may mean that some families are left out.

Some of the licensed programs choose a higher level of accreditation administered by national agencies. Some of these accreditation organizations and agencies include:

- National Association for the Education of Young Children (NAEYC)
- National Association for Family Child Care (NAFCC)
- National Early Childhood Program Accreditation (NECPA)
- Council on Accreditation (COA)

At the preschool level (ages 3 and 4), the delivery options include, but are not limited to:

- Public schools offering preschool services to all children or only in conjunction with early childhood special education programs
- Communities offering a coordinated, collaborative system of preschool services through the public schools, early education programs, and Head Start
- Local preschools (nonprofit or for-profit) offering 3- and 4-year-old programming
- Early childhood centers providing preschool and prekindergarten programming along with infant and toddler services

What does this kind of fragmentation mean for children and families? At a minimum, it sets the stage for confusion and families grappling to know the best options for their child and family situation. The median cost of care for a 4-year-old in center-based care is $8,600 and in home based care it is $7,150 annually (Committee for Economic Development, 2019). These figures have real impact on the daily lives of families and children. Why and whether we consider the early years of life as either an individual concern or a societal responsibility play a key role in building strong early childhood systems. The societal construct of early childhood varies across the globe. So how do the social perspectives and policies of early education in the United States compare with those in other countries?

EARLY CHILDHOOD EQUITY IN OTHER COUNTRIES

When we look at early education policies, we see that other countries have made greater investments in their youngest citizens. In many countries, education is seen as a lifelong learning continuum from birth onward, and funding for programs and teacher training, as well as professional respect, are extended to all age groups. We spotlight three examples of this approach.

Canada

Ontario, Canada, demonstrates a strong commitment to young children through its full-day, 2-year program for 4- and 5-year-olds. Highlights of this program include a collaborative instructional partnership between highly qualified early childhood educators and kindergarten teachers using a play- and inquiry-based curriculum. This initiative was informed by research high-lighting the importance of brain development, economic returns for society, and strong relationships between high-quality early education and life/school readiness (Becker & Mastrangelo, 2017).

New Zealand

In New Zealand, the early education curriculum was overhauled in 1996 to honor Indigenous ways of knowing, Te Whāriki (New Zealand Ministry of Education, 2018). Thus, the curriculum builds from Maori traditions rather than adding a cultural component onto the current developmental standards. This provides one example of authentically centering collaborative work based on Indigenous tradition and the unique cultural and linguistic strengths that families bring to educational contexts.

Finland

Finland is acknowledged on a global scale as having educational success across the developmental spectrum. This came to light primarily as students excelled on the Programme for International School Assessment (PISA), as highlighted in the documentary *Waiting for Superman* (Guggenheim, 2011). More recent-ly, however, the national policy may be narrowing to restrict access to early childhood education by requiring family member employment in order to qualify for full-day care. This signals a move from universalism to selectivity (Lundkvist, Nyby, Autto, & Nygard, 2017). Even with this shift, the overarching Finnish support for education centers the child and the needs of the family at an early stage in the life of the family.

Although the United Nations Convention on the Rights of the Child was ratified in 1990, at an international level there is still a struggle to define ac-cess and rights to equitable early education. In a recent study comparing six high-performing early education systems across the globe, Sharon Lynn Kagan (2019) found that the equity narrative is shifting to suggest that "services de-signed to meet children's diverse needs, should be a universal right" (p. 14). This signals support for a more equitable approach to early education beyond a system split between public and private access.

HAVE SOCIETAL ATTITUDES CHANGED IN THE UNITED STATES?

Inequity across gendered lines in pay and parental support provides one example of the slow nature of attitudinal change in the United States. It is believed that women are making strides in their professional life and inching toward equal pay and opportunity. However, for women who have young children, this progress is complicated by societal factors and expectations. According to Geiger, Livingstone, and Bialek of the Pew Research Center (2019), most U.S. mothers are married (68%) and nearly one-quarter (24%) are parenting on their own. About 9 million mothers with a child younger than 18 are living without a spouse or partner, which has real economic ramifications.

According to the National Center for Children in Poverty (Koball & Jiang, 2018), 45% of children under the age of 6 live in households with low income, and 23% live in poverty. The official poverty rate is 12.7%, based on the U.S. Census Bureau's 2016 estimates. In that year, an estimated 43.1 million Americans lived in poverty, and less than half of the children living in poverty attended public preschool programs (Barnett, 2010; Semega, Fontenot, & Kollar, 2017). The question becomes one of access, and the statistics show the need for early education and support for all families.

FAMILY PERSPECTIVE

I was thrilled to learn we were welcoming our first child and I could afford to stay home for the first year. As a same-sex couple, it wasn't until recently that we were legally recognized as a married couple. Yet, our fears of losing a job, being discriminated against in other ways, laws that allow people to not serve us or help us due to religious beliefs are still very real. I need to maintain my career credentials and remain viable in my profession; therefore, I had to return to work. It was demoralizing to realize my entire salary went to pay for care for the next 2 years as I worked full-time.

FUNDING DILEMMAS

There are efforts to fund early childhood programs and services; however, they are not nearly enough to change the system. State spending has increased substantially from $2.4 billion in 2002 to $8.1 billion in 2018 (Diffey, 2017). This may seem like a large increase; however, it is misleading if not adjusted for inflation. Around $2.4 billion was spent in 2002, but with adjustment for inflation this equals $3.9 billion. Therefore, in reality, the funding from 2002 to 2018 was just a bit more than double.

This phenomenon has been called "money illusion," leading to false conclusions about what may seem like gains, but are in actuality losses in real dollars (Diffey, 2017). For example, Friedman-Krauss et al. (2019) provide funding statistics for the 2017–2018 school year. Total state funding for preschool across 44 states and the District of Columbia was more than $8.15 billion; the per-child calculation equals $5,172. This included a small increase of $161 per child; however, when adjusted for inflation, it was reduced to $149 (a reduction of $12 per child). Friedman-Krauss et al. raise concerns that "unless state spending begins to grow faster, it will not be possible for states to make much progress in access, quality, or the provision of longer days" (p. 6).

Efforts are being made at the national level to fund preschool. Federal Preschool Development Grants (PDG) provided around $244 million during the 2017–2018 school year to states that qualified. Approximately $102 million of the PDG supported increased enrollment or quality enhancements in UPK. However, not all of this funding goes to sectors of the early childhood workforce (and the families it serves), which would benefit greatly by having this funding.

ECE CENTER OWNER PERSPECTIVE

I have been operating my program in this community for 23 years. My license is for children ages 6 weeks to 12 years. If my program cannot be part of the Universal Preschool collaboration, we will lose quite a lot of income from the 4-year-old classroom. Since infant and toddler care is more expensive (the ratio of adults to children is much lower), I am not sure I will be able to stay in business if I am not included in the collaboration. Needless to say, I am very worried about this possibility and so are many of the families who have their youngest children in my program.

Many economists have a voice in defending the importance of early education and are advocating that early childhood education is a sound investment that will result in returns in high school completion, strong workforce development, and later success in life (Sykes, 2014). Specific economic research forms a strong argument that funding preschool programming brings a significant return on investment (Heckman, Moon, Pinto, Savelyev, & Yavitz, 2010; Karoly, 2012; Kirp, 2007; Resnick, 2011) and that early education has positive impacts on later school success (Choi, Elicker, Christ, & Dobbs-Oates, 2016; Gormley, Phillips, & Gayer, 2008; Graf, Hernandez, & Bingham, 2016; Weiland & Yoshikawa, 2013; Wong, Cook, Barnett, & Jung, 2008).

Even with additional scientific and economic evidence of the value of early education, societal attitudes are slow to change. The lack of adequate funding, along with the fragmented approach, has dramatic impacts for the early childhood educational system in the United States (Berliner, 2006; Gilliam & Zigler, 2000; Parker, Keily, Atchison, & Mullen, 2019). Solutions to fund early education have ranged from federal allowances and state funding (Barnett & Kasmin, 2018; Gallagher, Clayton, & Heinemeir, 2001; Shaefer et al., 2018) to using private-sector investment to initiate change toward self-sustaining systems (Buffet Early Childhood Institute, 2013) and taxing the wealthiest citizens

GENERAL PUBLIC PERSPECTIVE

My employer offers an on-site early childhood center. At first, I didn't like that money was being spent on this benefit when I don't have children. However, now I see that my coworkers seem less stressed about where their children are every day, don't miss as many meetings, and seem more efficient at their jobs.

to support early education for all (Warren, 2019). The use of K–12 funding formulas is gaining traction as a way to create stable funding for Universal Preschool initiatives (Barnett & Kasmin, 2018). Another possible funding source at the local level involves employers contributing to their local community by finding ways to subsidize early care and education. This would move beyond the legislation to support families through dependent care tax credits and seek a more significant investment from the private sector.

Considering that early childhood programs continue to be grossly underfunded, families who can least afford to pay for quality services are left with few options. This has resulted in a patchwork of programs (both licensed and unlicensed) that families turn to, sometimes based on quality but most often based on price and geographic convenience. To further complicate this issue, early childhood professionals are woefully underpaid and undervalued (Interlandi, 2018; McLean, Dichter, & Whitebook, 2017; Whitebook & Ryan, 2012). This has led to a staffing crisis in the early childhood education profession that continues to impact the most vulnerable children and families (Barnett & Kasmin, 2017). How have we ended up in this situation?

THE EARLY CHILDHOOD PROFESSION

Many people agree that preschool provides a critical link to later formal schooling, and yet the early childhood profession is not widely recognized as an important, respected, formal field of study and practice. There are some parallels between early childhood and the nursing profession. For many years, nursing was considered primarily women's work, done in charity settings, with low pay and recognition. Nursing has achieved a high level of respect and status as the profession unionized, increased wages, and educated the public on the importance of its work. This development of the nursing profession became a national discussion, resulting in new standards, educational requirements, and oversight.

In Gilbert Steiner's 1976 book, *The Children's Cause*, the case was made for how the United States had failed to develop comprehensive policies and coordination of efforts for young children (Goffin, 2015). Since 1976, there

EC Professional Perspective

I have been in the early childhood education profession for over 35 years. Back in 1992, I participated in the very first Worthy Wage Day to call attention to the low wages of early childhood professionals, the effect those low wages have on recruitment and retention of staff, and the lack of public funding for early childhood programs and services. I find it a bit discouraging that 27 years later, we have not really made that much progress compared with other countries.

have been noble efforts to professionalize the early childhood field of practice; however, relatively slow progress has occurred and there remains a lack of consensus within the field.

A current initiative to increase the professional level of the early childhood workforce is called Power to the Profession (National Association for the Education of Young Children [NAEYC], 2016). It is being spearheaded by NAEYC in response to the Institute of Medicine and National Research Council's *Transforming the Workforce for Children Birth Through Age 8* report (2015). The report found a fragmented early childhood workforce in need of uniform qualifications, career pathways, and professional supports. This fragmentation is one of the major contributors to the varying levels of access to, and quality of, early childhood education programs throughout the country. Power to the Profession is an initiative to define the professional field of practice that unifies early childhood educators across all states and settings so they can further enrich the lives of children and families.

NAEYC identified a national taskforce of organizations that represent and engage large groups of early childhood professionals. The collaboration around this effort includes other national stakeholder organizations with systems-level influence on the profession. The plan includes holding virtual and local in-person town hall meetings. The hope is to allow early childhood educators and other experts to contribute their critical on-the-ground perspectives (NAEYC, 2016).

Teacher Perspective

I entered the early childhood profession because I was excited to have an impact on the development and growth of young children—I didn't realize that people I meet see me as a glorified babysitter and don't understand why my job is so important. There is little respect for my educational qualifications and dedicated work. It's hard to consider staying in this field when my work is not seen as important. Given my current salary and student loan debt, I'm worried that I'll fall below the poverty line!

SUMMARY

Reviewing the broader social constructs provides a frame for the deeper discussion of Universal Preschool in the United States. Given the mosaic of early childhood education policies, programs, funding, and governance, opening Universal Preschool as a public option for all young children requires strong collaborative approaches. This effort is complicated due to the variety of regulations, standards, and requirements that have evolved to oversee the diverse early education services provided by Head Start, child-care centers, and public schools (Friedman-Krauss et al., 2018). The need to communicate across the various agencies and organizations brings up issues of power structures, access, leadership, curricular philosophies, and funding sources. These issues remain constant factors in Universal Preschool and will be discussed in the remaining chapters.

REFLECTIVE CONVERSATIONS AND ACTIONS

1. What are your beliefs about how and where young children receive education and care services? How did you come to have these beliefs? What framed your thinking? How does the definition of family factor into early education and access?
2. What is your perspective on Universal Preschool in the United States? Do you think it should be fully funded by the government? If so, how? In not, why? In the era of creative personal fundraising, such as GoFundMe, what creative funding configurations could work? What are your experiences as a parent, grandparent, relative, friend, neighbor, or community member in relation to Universal Preschool?
3. Have you experienced or learned of early childhood systems in other countries? If so, what is your perspective on their effectiveness? If not, which countries would you be interested in learning more about? How does the ideology (democratic, socialist, communist) of a nation impact the formation and creation of educational systems?
4. What has been your experience in social situations when you reveal that you work in early childhood education or a related profession? In what ways does society value what you do? How could you respond to others to educate them about the value of ECE?
5. When discussing universal access, the question was raised regarding the difference between equal and equitable access. At the following link there is a worksheet to consider these ideas in relation to liberation: www.the4thbox.com. How might these ideas influence next steps in terms of your participation in the planning, creation, or implementation of Universal Preschool programs?

CHAPTER 2

Universal Preschool
Panacea or Perpetuated Patchwork

As we journey toward equity for early childhood education, Universal Preschool often is seen as the answer. Although it might be a step in the right direction for educational equity, it has implications for families and the broader birth-to-8 system. For example, all school districts are required to provide special education services to 3- and 4-year-old children. These districts may offer preschool services to children with disabilities along with their typically developing peers. Children who attended a community early childhood education program may now attend a preschool sponsored by the school district. This could result in lost revenues for the local early education and care programs, as 3- and 4-year-olds bring a higher percentage of income than infants and toddlers. It also could have an impact on the education and care options available to families of young children.

Improving understanding of Universal Preschool for the general populace is the first step in addressing the confusion over what might be beneficial for young children and families. This lack of understanding impacts policy and funding at the local, state, and federal levels. Following their review of media coverage of Universal Preschool in New York City, Delaney and Neuman (2018) suggest a need for fact-based information about classrooms, teaching, and preschool experiences for families so that they can make informed decisions. Defining for families what constitute quality approaches to early education is an emotional flashpoint, as each sector can find a way to praise or vilify the policy for universal access to education at younger ages.

EC SPECIAL EDUCATION TEACHER PERSPECTIVE

Our school district implemented a collaborative preschool program 2 years ago, in conjunction with the local early education providers and Head Start. The 3- and 4-year-old children with disabilities are doing so well in this situation. In many cases, children were able to stay with their current early education provider and keep that important relationship. At the same time, the speech therapist provided coaching and mentoring to the teachers at the early education program to help children reach their Individual Education Program (IEP) goals. It really was a win-win situation for everyone!

DEFINING UNIVERSAL PRESCHOOL

In the early childhood literature, Universal Preschool generally refers to access to public education for all 3- and 4-year-olds. This could mean half-day or full-day programs. The onus to create these programs has fallen on the states (Committee for Economic Development, 2002; Parker, Diffey, & Atchison, 2018, National Governors Association Center for Best Practices & Council of Chief State School Officers, 2010; Scott, 2005). Universal Preschool differs from Head Start in that these "universal" public programs are available to all children regardless of income, whereas in order to access Head Start the family must meet certain income requirements. By its nature, the tuition of Universal Preschool is free, but additional care may be necessary before and after the official hours of the preschool program. The physical location and staffing credentials may vary as well. Although Universal Preschool policies historically have been determined at the state level, these early childhood policy initiatives have implications for a national movement (Fuller, 2007; Gallagher, Clayton, & Heimemeir, 2001; Zigler, Gilliam, & Jones, 2006).

Arguments supporting Universal Preschool include, but are not limited to:

1. It will create equal learning opportunities for all 3- and 4-year-olds regardless of race, class, and income.
2. It will improve long-term academic achievement for all children.
3. It will reduce the fragmentation of early childhood systems (Barnett, Robin, Hustedt, & Schulman, 2003; Barnett, Brown, & Shore, 2004; Ewen, Blank, Hart, & Schulman, 2001; McCoy et al., 2017; U.S. Department of Health and Human Services, 2003; Zigler, Gilliam, & Barnett, 2011).

Arguments highlighting cautions for Universal Preschool include, but are not limited to:

1. Private early education centers will be put out of business, and public state or district programs will absorb Head Start.
2. Targeted programs are a better use of taxpayers' dollars.
3. It will create lower-quality programs due to lack of evaluation.
4. Universal Preschool is cost-prohibitive (Bailey, Duncan, Odgers, & Yu, 2017; Fuller, 2014; Whitehurst, 2014).

Additional research gives a mixed review, suggesting there are both gains and uncertainty regarding long-term academic impact (e.g., Lipsey, Hofer, Dong, Farran, & Bilbrey, 2013). The controversy surrounding universal access to preschool connects the issue of education as a public right with our cultural notion of family within society. As Beatty (1995) points out, "preschool programs function in the contested and shifting space at the intersection of the private family and public life" (p. x). Early childhood education policy rarely is outwardly acknowledged as contentious. Yet, focusing on this public/private intersection that Beatty refers to provides greater insight into the early childhood education policy process. Somewhat more than half of 3- and 4-year-olds in the United States attend a preschool program, and 59% of those children attend a public program such as a state pre-K program (Siskel Jacobs Productions, 2018). State pre-K enrollment increased significantly from 2002 to 2014, and in 2014, approximately 40% of 4-year-olds and 12% of 3-year-olds were enrolled in public programs (Barnett, Weisenfeld, et al., 2016). As kindergarten has moved out of this spotlight, preschool education has taken its place in the debate over whether education of 3- and 4-year-olds is a private or public issue. This shifting terrain makes the early childhood education debate often emotional and passionate.

The National Education Association (NEA, 2019) states that high-quality early education represents one of the best investments our country can make—calling it a commonsense investment. The NEA advocates for free, publicly funded, high-quality kindergarten in all states; optional free, publicly funded, quality "universal" prekindergarten programs, especially for children living in poverty; and dedicated funding for early childhood education through public schools. However, if we suggest universal support for preschool, how do we ensure that it meets the needs of each unique child and family?

The United States has reached a point where public education for all citizens is a right, starting at the state-determined compulsory school attendance age. However, there are large differences between how early education and preschool are funded compared with the K–12 system (Friedman-Krauss et al., 2019). Forty-three states, plus the District of Columbia, use general revenues, with about 15 of those requiring a local match. Many states also rely on sales tax, lotteries, and general or gaming revenues to supplement school funding. While increased funding for Universal Preschool through public schools is a good start, it can be fraught with the mindset of increasing "3rd-grade reading scores" rather than providing developmentally appropriate and culturally relevant services and programming in the preceding years.

KEY COMPONENTS OF EARLY CHILDHOOD PROGRAMS

Studies typically outline the timeline, participants, and components of early education programs, as well as the key players in the development of the programs, and roadblocks and/or successes. Although these reports originate from separate studies, the general conclusions drawn from the data outline some of the same concerns and shortcomings for early childhood programs:

1. Fragmentation of programming
2. Insufficient or mixed funding sources
3. Difficulties of data collection
4. The ambiguous nature of quality

CONVERSATION AT A COMMUNITY EARLY CHILDHOOD POLICY MEETING

The topic is the implementation of the collaborative pilot program for 4-year-olds in one Head Start classroom and two district classrooms.

Molly: So let me get this straight, we are providing transportation but only in our attendance area.

Sara: Correct.

Lila: Well, wait a minute. I just saw the schedule. The class meets on Mondays from 7:45 to 9:52. Where do these kids go at 10A.M. then?

Sara: Home.

Lila: But 70% of this population is considered "low income," and with our welfare-to-work program, we know parents should be working.

Sara: Look, this isn't perfect, but it's a start. Families know how to work the system and they will figure this out, too. Hey, this is a free, voluntary program. If it doesn't fit their needs, it doesn't fit their needs. They can find another program.

Lila: Like what?

Molly: Like our Head Start program.

Lila: Okay, but didn't you just say this particular Head Start is a half-day site?

Molly: Yes.

Lila: I am not sure how this helps then, or how families are simply going to "figure this out."

Sara: No one said this would be perfect, but it's a start and the most important piece at this point is to prove that the kids' social, emotional, and academic skills improve based on this free access to education. We'll just have to work out the details as we go. The reality is we have the support and money to get this going and we need to get children registered in 2 weeks. Although I understand that these are important issues, we have to get practical here.

POLICYMAKER PERSPECTIVE

I have constituents who contact me every day about the high cost of early childhood services for their child. These families plead for more funding for Universal Preschool. They find it hard to balance work, finances, and the best interests of their child. I am committed to helping them.

From analysis of studies specific to 4-year-old programming, as well as other studies related to early childhood education and childhood outcomes (Barnett, Weisenfeld, et al., 2016; Bredekamp, Knuth, Kunesh, & Shulman, 1992; Frede, 1995; Friedman-Krauss et al., 2018; Minervino, 2014; Reynolds, Temple, Robertson, & Mann, 2001; Reynolds, Wang, & Walberg, 2003; Sachs, 2000), a number of key components have resonated as guides to success for early education programs (see Figure 2.1).

Figure 2.1. Key Components of and Recommendations for Early Education Programs

Key Component	Examples	Recommendations
Access	Universal versus a focus on "at-risk" populations	A suggested move to universal access and an offer of less fragmented services by providing transportation, flexible hours, and language support
Collaboration	Although most studies illustrate programs centered in public school systems, most programs required collaborative agreements with Head Start and private child-care agencies.	Provision of government support (legislative endorsement), political leaders' visible support, clear communication and participation with key players (Head Start, school districts, private providers), simplification of fragmented systems
Funding	Use of lottery money, a tobacco tax, federal incentives for quality	Requirement for multiple and stable sources of funding
Quality (related to staff)	Multiple definitions were recognized (teacher training, environment, curriculum, class size and ratio, etc.). Success of students was linked to "quality" of programming.	Refining the definition of quality; more accountability for the quality of programs
Program evaluation (framework for maintaining and monitoring programs)	Recognition of inaccurate collection of data regarding state statistics for children served	Consistent data collection before, during, and after program implementation; improvement in state reporting regarding 3- and 4-year-olds
Staff support (related to quality)	Recognition of varying standards for teacher and assistant credentialing and training	Continuing education, increased compensation, professional recognition

These components represent how research is framing Universal Preschool with a focus on access, collaboration, funding, quality, program evaluation, and staff support. Although the research outlines definitive components of success, these guidelines for early childhood policy will be interpreted in various ways when implemented, leading to variations in what they truly "look like" in the classroom. Therefore, "success" depends on how the policy is read and interpreted and who has access to policy at different stages (Ball, 1994).

This overview of findings from current Universal Preschool initiatives highlights the complexity of policy creation. In this book, we take the component of collaboration and explore the impact on one past UPK pilot and the present efforts and trends in Universal Preschool policy initiatives across the United States.

UNIVERSAL PRESCHOOL EFFORTS REQUIRE COLLABORATION

Collaboration is a term frequently used within the field of education. A variety of service and delivery options for Universal Preschool initiatives has created heightened interest in collaboration in early education (Selden, Sowa, & Sandfort, 2006). What does it actually mean in a Universal Preschool context? How does the act of collaboration happen on a level playing field when a variety of individuals and organizations come to the table? While we focus on the complexities of collaboration, power, and discourse in Universal Preschool, we continue to recognize that preschool exists in a wider context of programs and services for families with children under 3 years of age and the K–12 educational system.

Economically creative and collaboratively inclusive international approaches, as highlighted in Chapter 1, provide insight for alternative ECE policy pathways in the United States (Lubeck, 2001). However, the reality of our existing political constructs, dictating the nation's educational funding streams, frames our work for collaborative ECE approaches. For example, adding universal access at the 4-year-old level does not necessarily suggest interagency collaboration. Too often, preschool is "added on" to existing K–12 schools, with the danger of pushing down curriculum, versus creating relevant approaches for young children (Berner, 2016; Brown & Gasko, 2012; Wilinski, 2017b).

WHAT DOES COLLABORATION HAVE TO DO WITH POLICY?

Policy is not simply a text to read, follow, or debate. Within every context where the policy is used, it is interpreted, re-created, and altered in specific ways. According to Ball (1994), policy is both a process and an outcome. There are multiple ways that policy is defined, used, and positioned in social settings. He

FAMILY PERSPECTIVE

As a child I attended Head Start. It wasn't just preschool; it was my community, my extended family. Now, in our community, we have the option to choose a public program for Zoe when she turns 4. Does this mean that children who might attend Head Start will instead have to go to preschool at a public school? What will happen to Head Start funding and the comprehensive services that they offer children and families? So many families benefit from the Head Start approach to the whole child and family. Will these same services be offered to all children in a universal preschool model? Even though our family does not qualify for Head Start right now, that could easily change with economic circumstances. I am in favor of universal preschool; however, I don't want to see other good preschool programs suffer in the process.

articulates two versions of policy: policy as text and policy as discourse. These versions are "implicit in each other" (p. 15). The policies attached to Universal Preschool include, but are not limited to, access, funding, and leadership. These policies frame the protocols and practices around important components of a program, such as curriculum, transportation, and enrollment. Collaboration at some level is required in Universal Preschool as many agencies currently offer ECE programs.

For Ball (1994), a policy text is read and interpreted and as such is never "clear or closed or complete. . . . [It is] the product of compromises at various stages" of policy development, negotiation, and interpretation (p. 16). "Policies *are* textual interventions into practice" (p. 18, emphasis in original). Practice is determined by a reading and interpretation of the policy. For example, teachers read and implement (or perhaps do not) a particular curriculum policy, while at the same time they negotiate how policy poses problems that must be resolved in context. In other words, policy does not determine practice, but it does limit the options available and the possible outcomes. So, policy matters.

Policy is not a static text but gains power through its enactment by teachers, administrators, and families. Enactment of policy does not happen in a vacuum and therefore requires communication among key stakeholders. Collaboration often is defined as a coming together of interested individuals to work on a common project. With the continuing expansion of publicly funded Universal Preschool, collaboration is being touted as a method to ensure that high-quality preschool programs are implemented successfully in local settings. Collaboration in this sense refers to the bringing together of various program types (Head Start, public schools, child care) that for the most part have operated alongside, rather than with, one another (Barnett, 2010).

Research evidence and literature indicate that if the expansion of preschool programs is to harness the benefits associated with high-quality model programs, fragmented systems have to be simplified; this requires communication

PRINCIPAL PERSPECTIVE

As a principal in the district, I have the responsibility of working within a set budget and addressing professional development required by the district. I see this policy as limited yet required. I am reviewed based on meeting these budget goals and following what the district has laid out as priorities. Often, funding is earmarked for initiatives that don't align with my community. How do I honor what I have learned from the community about their needs and reconcile that with what the district requires?

and participation of all stakeholders within a community (Bredekamp et al., 1992; Kagan & Gomez, 2015; Reynolds et al., 2003; Schulman & Blank, 2009). The danger of this approach is an oversimplification of the needs of children and families in diverse and disparate situations.

PANDORA'S BOX OF POWER/KNOWLEDGE RELATIONSHIPS

One of the goals of this book is to look at early childhood policy and practice in a new light, taking into consideration larger discourses as well as individual interpretations of the process. Use of a critical perspective provides some explanation for how this disconnection between perceived intent and practice occurs. Critical theory suggests the need to acknowledge the inherent complications in addressing universal needs of a pluralistic society that span its public and private spheres. Therefore, we continue to clarify as well as question the early childhood policy process in relation to the creation of Universal Preschool programs and what that might mean for administrators, community members, teachers, children, and families. Although one or more goals may be attached to a policy, there is elasticity and translation around the work, which could be defined as interpretation and enactment. The elasticity and translation create hybrids of the policy (Derrida, 1978). Universal Preschool policy shifts based on perspective and the discourse shaping the policy. We create a balance of recognition of the discursive forces at play and offer suggestions and explorations to address equity and access in early education. We hope that through telling complicated stories, new insights into the process might be gleaned.

We define the discourses and truths embedded in policy, and question how these discourses manifest themselves in the lives of people working in the field of early childhood education policy. In addition, we consider the invasive nature of power, specifically in relation to the inclusion or exclusion of individuals in the Universal Preschool policy process. A deeper consideration is offered of the notion that power is circulating and that individuals use their authorized power to reinforce discourses (Foucault, 1980). This results in a closer look at policy theory, discourse, and power/knowledge relationships that circulate in collaborative efforts.

Foucault's theoretical position rests on the notion that power is circulating; it influences and is influenced by knowledge. Unlike a sovereign notion of power (e.g., hierarchical, a birthright, imposed), Foucault suggests that there is both a systemic form of power and an individual enactment of power. Through this individual enactment of power, the larger "net-like" power structures may be either reinforced or resisted (Foucault, 1980, p. 98). For example, an educator may feel empowered to uniquely implement the curriculum, and yet that educator is evaluated by how well the students perform on standardized assessments. In relation to this, discipline is seen as both an external and internal function of power (e.g., the panopticon) (Foucault, 1995). Therefore, this internal discipline or technology of the self (Martin, Gutman, & Hutton, 1988) suggests that individuals monitor themselves in society; however, this monitoring also is influenced by the available discourses that either constrain or facilitate their actions. In addition, we consider other disciplinary techniques, such as funding support (or the lack of funding) for collaboration. This could be viewed as an external disciplinary technique to reinforce the discourse that true collaboration is possible. Money is being supplied to fund the collaborative initiative, so success through collaborative work must be attainable. In this way, power is not seen as good or bad. In applying Foucault's ideas, we acknowledge in these stories that power can be "dangerous" and therefore should be questioned and challenged (Rabinow, 1984). Through ongoing critique, relevance of policy across time and contexts is possible.

While many efforts have been made to outline comprehensive early childhood services, the practical application of offering collaborative services relies on strong partnerships and collaboration at the local level. Aligning the multiple perspectives of key stakeholders in early education with fragmented early education systems is at the heart of understanding the complexity of a collaborative approach.

COLLABORATION AS DISCOURSE

Discourse is seen "as practices that systematically form the objects of which they speak" (Foucault, as cited in Ball, 1994, p. 21). There is a dynamic of power

EC DIRECTOR PERSPECTIVE

I need a degree in business to keep this school afloat. In the best-case scenario, my choices are to join a corporate chain, partner with a school district or Head Start, or remain an autonomous small business. I rely on tuition to offset expenses, and as a small business owner I cannot afford the benefits these teachers deserve. I apply for soft money initiatives and local grants, but barely break even. The balance of meeting safety and health requirements for our children and keeping the school running is a daily dilemma.

relationships (most often hidden) at work that constructs certain meanings around a policy and how it is interpreted and enacted. Discourses also determine individual access to the process in terms of power and capital. Forms of capital include financial as well as social and cultural (Bourdieu, 1977). That is, even when individuals are invited to collaborate in the process of formulating early childhood education policies, some, because of their position and status, have more say than others. The discourses at work in a policy setting determine who is included, who gets to speak, and whose voice is heard.

> Discourse ... is itself produced by a practice: "discursive practice"—the practice of producing meaning. Since all social practices entail *meaning*, all practices have a discursive aspect. So, discourse enters into and influences all social practices. (Hall & Gieben, 1992, p. 291, emphasis in original)

In other words, discourse is not a simple set of words, but it is through the "discursive practice" or action that meaning is created. Therefore, by considering these practices in relation to the message or meaning they are sending, we see a formation begin to take shape (Foucault, 1972). The notion and use of developmentally appropriate practice (DAP) representing what is considered "best practice" in ECE symbolizes a regularity—it has come to be expected in our early education programs.

However, these practices may leave room for interpretation based on the beliefs and mental models of early childhood practitioners. Hall and Gieben (1992) summarize their discussion of discourse by suggesting that:

> Discourses are ways of talking, thinking or representing a particular subject or topic. They produce meaningful knowledge about that subject. This knowledge influences social practices, and so has real consequences and effects. ... The question of whether a discourse is true or false is less important than whether it is effective in practice. When it is effective—organizing and regulating relations of power ... —it is called a "regime of truth." (p. 295)

TERMINOLOGY TIPS

Developmentally appropriate practice is an approach to teaching grounded in the research suggesting that children develop and learn along milestones of development in social–emotional, physical, and cognitive domains. DAP involves teachers meeting young children where they are, both as individuals and as part of a group, and helping each child meet challenging and achievable learning goals based on these milestones. Three core areas of knowledge guide DAP practices: (1) knowing about child development and learning; (2) knowing what is individually appropriate; and (3) knowing what is culturally important (NAEYC, 2009).

The discussion around DAP provides a link to understanding the importance of discourse. The "practice" appears to become normalized and accepted as a "truth" when it becomes an effect of power and knowledge through a discursive practice. Therefore, DAP becomes known as a "truth." As knowledge and contexts shift across time, it is important to critique and question our practices. There are other examples that we will explore where discourses become interpreted as "truths." These include "universal access" and "community collaboration" as solutions for ECE policy dilemmas in Universal Preschool (Foucault, 1972). For example, often funding (such as early learning opportunity grants, Race to the Top Early Learning Challenge, preschool expansion grants, preschool development grants, and others) granted to agencies and organizations is based on the contingency that more than one entity (e.g., Head Start, public schools) will benefit from the program, thus emphasizing the need to acquire or exhibit skills in collaborative policymaking. The implication is that including multiple programs will ensure collaboration. Critiquing the discourse of collaboration is helpful to assess the inclusion, authenticity, and level of engagement of partners.

A COLLABORATIVE APPROACH

We define collaboration as a multi-agency (multi-stakeholder) policy process in which shared decisionmaking, costs, leadership, goals, and equity of input are implied. The idea that equity is implied in the definition signals that the nature of the process becomes less about equity in sharing and more about realizing power differentials and negotiating limitations.

Collaborative or community approaches to Universal Preschool have become popular options in efforts to include all stakeholders while capitalizing on existing community resources (Casto, Sipple, & McCabe, 2014; Goble & Horm, 2009; Reynolds et al., 2003; Selden et al., 2006; U.S. Government Accountability Office, 2004). This collaborative approach to policymaking is seen as working within the democratic spirit of our nation, allowing key stakeholders the opportunity to be heard (Sandfort & Selden, 2001). Early in the Universal Preschool movement (before 2005), the majority of state-sponsored preschool programs were opting for what was referred to as a "mixed delivery model" that included private community centers, Head Start, and public school sites (Schumacher, Hamm, & Ewen, 2007). Collaborations, whether in the past or present, must occur among the existing stakeholders in the community: families, child-care centers, faith-based programs, school districts, Head Start sites, and other agencies. Funding sources and goals among these stakeholders vary. Many funded initiatives (e.g., preschool expansion grants, Race to the Top, PDG B-5, etc.) target improved early childhood policies and systems to assist with collaboration and program development. With a newly emerging body of research and literature exploring

FAMILY PERSPECTIVE

Ezra has been with Grow with Me Preschool since he was 10 months old. We feel connected to the center staff, and Tiffany in particular is like family. But I know there is a class at the neighborhood elementary school next year that would be free for us when he turns 4. It's hard to leave "our family," but free is hard to beat. Yet, I work full-time and the free program is only half days. I just don't know what's best for Ezra.

Universal Preschool collaborative efforts (Casto et al., 2014; Wilinski, 2017b), we hope the concepts, ideas, and discussions offered throughout this book will enhance collaborative efforts for all stakeholders.

In response to concerns over closing the achievement gap and meeting the educational needs of all 4-year-olds, the notion of creating collaborations or community partnerships has become part of the solution. For some, a collaborative approach to offering 4-year-old educational programs is a panacea for many of our educational concerns. This implies that teachers, principals, and administrators of multiple agencies actively communicate or "collaborate" and share information and resources. It is assumed that co-leaders and shared governance will emerge among the parties involved. However, this is not always the case.

Seddon, Billett, and Clemans (2005) suggest, in the *British Journal of Sociology of Education*, that the current research outlines collaboration either in optimistic terms ("a panacea") or as critiques that highlight exclusionary tactics of neo-liberal governance. They seek a middle road and suggest using research to inform the policy process regarding the experiences of partnerships. Their analysis is helpful as we consider the Universal Preschool movement. They describe three common partnership models:

1. *Enacted partnerships* are initiated by external agencies but have goals of relevance to, or shared by the community....
2. *Community partnerships* originate in the community to address local concerns but reach out to external agencies to secure adequate resources and support for dealing with identified problems or issues ...
3. *Negotiated partnerships* are formed between partners with reciprocal goals to secure a service or support and required effective negotiation of interests and agenda. (pp. 576–577).

Universal Preschool collaborative initiatives most often fit in the first model, "enacted partnerships," in which external agencies (school districts) share goals with the community. However, there is potential to frame the Universal Preschool movement using any one of these models. The alternative to a collaborative approach is too often an add-on ECE program to existing public K–12 programs—running the risk of pushing down academics. Therefore, there is an interest and a need to further investigate the experience and construction of collaboration or partnerships (Wilinski, 2017a).

COLLABORATIVE LEADERSHIP

In much of the recent literature, collaborative leadership is seen as a participatory process based on democratic notions of shared responsibility. This body of scholarship pulls from systems theory models from the business field. However, unlike traditional hierarchical models, it is founded on the belief that answers to complex organizational issues are found in community, and people, as well as organizations, that are always learning (Senge, 1990; Wheatley, 1992):

> A basic premise of collaborative leadership is the recognition that no one person has the solutions to the multifaceted problems that a group or organization must address. Leadership in this context requires **a set of principles** that empower all members to act, and employ a process that allows the collective wisdom to surface. These principles must be based on an understanding that people have the knowledge and creativity to respond to the problems they face. They encourage the development of organizations to support collective action based on shared vision, ownership, and mutual values. (Allen et al., 1997, p. 4, bold in the original)

The core principles of this model include the idea of fostering shared power (Allen et al., 1997). These principles, while helpful, remain ambiguous (Lockwood, 1996). Studies considering collaborative leadership in policy (Honig, 2003; Ryan, 2001) suggest that generating a "collaborative process" takes a certain amount of education and coaching. Emphasis is placed on the need to recognize different types of expertise across the "hierarchy" in current educational administration programs (Honig, 2003). In education, there is some interest in applying collaborative leadership concepts within school sites, with outcomes suggesting a positive influence on student learning (e.g., Burch & Spillane, 2004; Hallinger & Heck, 2010). In early childhood education, the increasing need for collaborative leadership is acknowledged, including a focus on the strengths of teachers in individual settings and across the field of education (Douglass, 2017; Rodd, 2012).

The pragmatics of collaboration benefit from specific ideas and examples. Directives suggest that collaborative leadership requires an openness to others' values, priorities, and circumstances, as well as sharing responsibility and costs equitably. Subsequent trust will enhance respectful communication around the development of roles and responsibilities, and ultimately foster shared leadership and decisionmaking (Arts Consulting Group, 2003; Chrislip, 2002; Strauss, 2002).

These ideas fit into a more optimistic rendering of collaboration, suggesting that with training and support, a collaborative initiative will be successful. However, this approach to collaborative leadership does not address the critique that collaboration is a neo-liberal construction that seeks to create a false sense of empowerment for individuals and agencies in order to fulfill a larger political agenda. We address collaboration in terms of a middle ground between these two interpretations (Seddon et al., 2005). This middle ground allows for engagement while maintaining a critical view of the potential to prioritize a political agenda. We describe how teachers function in UPK collaborations, using curriculum policy as a way to explore collaborative leadership (Chapter 5). These examples provide concrete ways to consider the impact of larger agency discourses and power relationships (Foucault, 1980).

THE EARLY CHILDHOOD COLLABORATIVE (ECC): PAST STORIES OF UPK

Viewing the policy, power, and discourse of collaboration through a historical case study brings real-life perspective to the study of the inception of Universal Preschool. We now turn to the context of the "Past" stories to bring collaboration to life. These stories are based on a case study in a school district 15 years ago. Data were gathered from 2001 to 2004, following the process from policy formulation to implementation. All names of individuals, organizations, and places are fictional, and any connection with real names would be accidental. First names are used to facilitate readability.

The ECC is located in Arborville, a medium-sized midwestern city in the United States. Arborville is seen as a family-friendly city, having received several awards that include best city for families and best small city for women. The city enjoys national prestige as a supportive environment for women, children, and families, as well as having National Schools of Excellence. Given this reputation, the news that the public kindergarten for "at-risk" (generally understood to mean lower-SES and/or special needs) 4-year-old children was ending, came as a surprise to most of the local early childhood community. The program served approximately 168 students. The reason given for canceling the program of 30 years was that the district, in operating the program for a targeted population, was no longer in compliance with the state's universal access provision.

The historical and cultural context of the state with regard to kindergarten and 4-year-old programming is important to consider. This state was one of the first to provide universal access to kindergarten, and also has a provision in its constitution for universal access to 4-year-old kindergarten. Attendance in 4K in this state peaked in the 1920s; in the 1950s, state funding was cut for these programs. Baby boomers were reaching school age at this time, and one might suggest, based on the need for classrooms for the growing population of school-age children, that preschool children were crowded out. Following this major shift in state funding, districts chose whether or not to implement 4K.

In 1980, this state's education department created a 4K task force to consider the issues statewide. Although there was an interest in addressing the issues surrounding 4K, in this district the schools were independent yet had cross-pollination of programming (Head Start, public school, private providers) starting in the early 1980s. Through the 1980s and 1990s, essentially there was an unspoken agreement that everyone would stay within their territorial boundaries. As early as 1989, it was recommended that districts consider collaborations between schools, child care, Head Start, and families to create programs to offer care for all 4-year-olds. However, until the news of the cancellation, no major changes had been made to the Arborville program for 4-year-olds.

While six districts within the state had already started to follow community-based approaches to 4-year-old public schooling programs, in the same academic year (2000–2001), Arborville was offering public preschool primarily through Head Start—a federal program that serves lower-income families. As the state required that public education be universally available, the district administration had to create a new form of public preschool program.

According to the state's education department, 43% of the school districts statewide had UPK programs as of November 2003. If the ECC initiative was passed by Arborville's school board, it potentially would serve 1,800 4-year-old children in the district, some of whom were already being served through the previous program for "at-risk" children. Based on the district's past interest in UPK and the growing number of districts and children being served, the climate seemed conducive for exploring collaborative options for a new UPK program.

Following the news that the existing "at-risk" 4K program would end, forums were coordinated and, as time passed, a core group of interested community members began to meet and plan on a regular basis. The group consisted primarily of district administrators, teachers, and center directors. The goal of this group was to consider a collaborative effort (between Head Start, city child-care offices, the school district, and the local university) to meet the needs of 4-year-olds in Arborville using existing programs as well as newly created partnerships. Basically, four different service options were created to better meet the needs of families: public school sites, child-care sites, family care sites, and public school staff in community sites. These options also allowed for families already enrolled in child-care programs to potentially remain with their provider. By having these options, and through the work of partnerships, the initiative hoped to avoid decimating existing quality child-care programs. The work of this planning group at this time included creating policy to frame and define participants, funding, curriculum, teachers, transportation, and communication to the community.

This process continued for almost 2 years, culminating in a presentation to the school board requesting funding for a collaborative 4-year-old kindergarten.

The state funding required 3 years of local start-up money before the state money would become available to the new program. Given other financial demands on the school board, the proposal was tabled. Following this decision, there was concern that the collaborative effort and the ECC would be abandoned.

Finally, the news story broke that the school board had approved a partnership with the Abbott Center (a university research group) and the district to create a pilot UPK program with Greentree Elementary. Head Start also would become a partner in this pilot as planning took place. Partial funding offered by the Abbott Center made this pilot program possible.

There were two classrooms: one at the Head Start site (Waterfront) and the other at Greentree Elementary. Demographics indicate both sites were located in racially and economically diverse neighborhoods. The sites were approximately 2 miles from each other, so they shared school attendance areas. However, the Head Start site was located in a converted duplex in a subsidized housing neighborhood where the children lived. The classroom in the elementary school was located on the lower level next to the cafeteria, and across from the early childhood program for children with special needs. Each classroom had 14 to 17 children with one teacher and one assistant. The Waterfront site served only one group of children in the morning, while the Greentree site had both morning and afternoon classes.

In Chapters 3, 4, and 5, we continue to explore the "Past" story of the ECC, focusing on the planning of a pilot UPK program. The stories focus on the dynamics of policy and power within the collaborative efforts. Each story looks at a different aspect of the collaboration. Chapter 3 looks at the community meetings that explored Universal Preschool. Chapter 4 delves into issues of

Together

enrollment and equitable access to UPK. Chapter 5 explores the underlying issues of leadership and beliefs around curriculum.

SUMMARY

When individuals and agencies enter into a collaborative relationship to provide Universal Preschool, there are many issues to work through in a mutually agreeable manner. These issues can include, but are not limited to, funding, enrollment, staff, curriculum, child assessment, family engagement, and transportation. Positional and organizational power differentials create obstacles when finding mutual agreement in these areas. Some voices will dominate, while other individuals/groups may feel disempowered. Through telling these "Past" UPK stories, stepping back to frame each story using the notion of power, offering updated "Present" vignettes, and inserting unique perspectives from the community represented in the stories, we offer insights on policy decisions and apply these insights to future undertakings for Universal Preschool.

REFLECTIVE CONVERSATIONS AND ACTIONS

1. In what ways does deeply thinking about the concepts of power, knowledge, trust, and perspective relate to your own collaborative experiences? How do these concepts play out in your life on a daily basis?
2. What policies may help or hinder collaboration across early childhood systems? Are there standards, regulations, outcomes, or other policies that lead to confusion around what is best for young children and families? In what ways have you been involved in policy discussions around ECE at the local, state, or national level? Additional resources are available in the Early Care and Education Collaboration: A Key Topic Resource List at *www.researchconnections.org/childcare/resources/22863?publisher=Child+Care+%26+Early+Education+Research+Connections&q=&paging.rows=100&sortBy=1&classifCode=8#*.
3. Creating Universal Preschool programs as either "add-ons" to existing public K–12 programs or as community partnerships raises a variety of dilemmas. In what ways do power and discourse shape the options? How do history, funding, and societal values influence the policy in your community?
4. Has there been a time in your personal or professional life that you have been part of a collaboration? What was your role? Do you feel that you were heard? What would have made the collaboration more effective? How might the three partnership models inform your answer?
5. What opportunities do you see in your personal or professional life to be part of a new collaboration? What could you do as an individual to promote the importance of early childhood programs and services in our society?

CHAPTER 3

Encouraging All Voices in the Universal Preschool Conversation

In many ways, the policy emphasis on collaboration as a means of ensuring the implementation of high-quality systems of preschool education seems like a sensible goal. After all, it makes good sense for families to be able to locate and access preschool in their local communities, knowing that it will be of high quality and similar to other programs regardless of auspices. To be successfully accepted, any top-down policy initiative requires the buy-in and input of stakeholders. It also seems logical to involve community members in the policy formulation process. Antonio Novoa writes that collaboration fits into what he calls "planetspeak" or "banalities universally accepted as truth that have no known origin and do not need to be questioned" (Franklin, Bloch, & Popkewitz, 2003, pp. 3–4). Despite the promise of collaboration, early childhood policies will not be responsive to the communities they serve without some reconsideration of how collaboration is defined and enacted. If collaboration is to be successful, a variety of proactive strategies should be considered.

COLLABORATIVE POLICY

[handwritten annotation: How was this viewed by teacher in my study (were they even able to) imp this level?]

Instead of bringing together communities under the pretense of eliciting their perspectives, efforts must be made to develop the social capital of marginalized groups and document local efforts to make change. While there is no utopian or "right" way to create preschool policy, by acknowledging the politics and power of the process, it may be possible to develop programs that meet the needs of those they serve. In order to bring diverse voices to the table, alternative ways of creating space for participants in policy formulation need to be considered. It is in these spaces that possibilities exist to create and present counternarratives to dominant views of how collaborative early childhood education should be enacted.

In the "Past" story, we explore specific policy interactions of one UPK collaborative—the issues of who was included, the capital needed for inclusion, the power related to social networks, and how these factors shape collaboration. The "Present" story explores a contemporary example of policy and inclusion at community levels and mirrors insights from the "Past" story.

PAST STORY: ECC—VOICES AT THE TABLE

"From the beginning, invite everyone."

—Arborville Department of Education

The overview of the Early Childhood Collaborative provided in Chapter 2 lays the foundation for this portion of the story—dealing with policy formulation and community engagement. The Arborville School District (ASD) was under pressure to discontinue the existing system of offering access to preschool to "at-risk" 4-year-old children and implement a universally available preschool program. Therefore, district administration had to create another form of public preschool if it was to offer public schooling for 4-year-olds at all. To get the process started, the ASD administration hired two part-time consultants to explore the needs of the community. This was the birth of the ECC in this community.

The policy formulation process in Arborville was enacted through collaboration between representatives of the school district, Head Start, the city office for child care, and community child-care centers. David Smith (Arborville School District consultant) set the tone of this process early on at one of the first early childhood community meetings:

> Welcome, everyone, to the first gathering of individuals interested in creating new possibilities for our 4-year-old children in Arborville. We are glad to have you join us for this journey we are embarking on. We are hoping to challenge ourselves as a group to consider a total paradigm shift to help us maintain the "big picture" as we work together. We would like to begin by going around the circle today and introducing ourselves. Please state your name, your position in the community, and why you are here.

Participants were recruited through community meetings like the one above. As time passed, a core group of interested community members began to meet and plan a collaborative effort (including Head Start, city child-care offices, the school district, and the local university) to meet the educational needs of 4-year-olds in Arborville using existing programs as well as newly created partnerships.

Developing a Vision

The vision of the ECC generated by this group was succinct: "ECC is a comprehensive high-quality early learning system that meets the developmental needs of all young children in the Arborville area" (Arborville School District, 2002). Basically, four different service options were created to better meet the needs of families:

1. Half-day preschool in at least one public school classroom, with wrap-around care available through local child-care services
2. Half-day preschool in local community child-care programs, staffed by teachers recruited by the ASD
3. Half-day preschool provided under ASD contract with community-based child-care programs, with programs recruiting certified teachers to teach preschool
4. Community-based and accredited family child-care programs, with certified teachers providing in-home preschool

With all of these options, the Arborville School District was to provide special education services and other support services (e.g., transportation) as needed. Using these options and working as partners, the ECC hoped to avoid decimating existing quality early childhood education programs, while at the same time ensuring that families already enrolled in child-care programs potentially could stay with their provider. Figure 3.1 presents the details of these four options.

EC DIRECTOR PERSPECTIVE

I've heard rumors that Universal Preschool is going to grow in this area. What does that mean for our enrollment? Our sole source of income is tuition, and if we lose the 4-year-olds who balance the cost of our infant care, I'm afraid we'll go out of business.

The preschool proposal of the ECC was presented at the ASD school board meeting in December 2002 and tabled due to budgetary needs. In addition, the school board raised concerns regarding the composition of the ECC committee. The board asked the ECC to develop a plan to include nonaccredited centers and family day care providers, and to find ways to ensure that the perspectives of all of Arborville's demographic groups were gathered. The final comment in the email written in 2003 by Sally Clinger (chair of the ECC) included the following:

As stated earlier and confirmed at the BOE [board] meeting, our group needs to represent the diverse population of Arborville . . . and we don't. It is critical to have multiple voices at the table, because each of us, as we have learned, sees the world through our own operating lens. I encourage you to make contacts with your networks, so that our community is well represented in this important, collaborative initiative.

Figure 3.1. Early Childhood Collaborative Delivery Models

OPTION I Public School Staff/ School Site	OPTION II Public School Staff/ Community Site	OPTION III Contracted Services/ Community Site	OPTION IV Contracted Services/Family Child-Care Home Site
Option IA: One classroom • A.M. and P.M. classes (2.5 hours each, school year) provided by district staff • Children will be enrolled based on living in school attendance area or parents working in attendance area, or other reasons. • Children are not enrolled in an early education and care program for any other part of the day.	• A.M. and P.M. classes (2.5 hours each, school year) • Public school teacher works within existing part-day or full-day community early childhood site. • Site may or may not be city/nationally accredited, but must be working on accreditation.	• Community sites (center-based programs, Head Start, family child care, part-day preschool programs) will have their own 4-year-degreed/licensed teacher. • Sites would need to hold NAEYC/City of Arborville accreditation and meet Head Start performance standards. • Funds could be contracted on a per-child basis, so sites could serve any number of eligible 4-year-olds.	• Community family sites will have their own 4-year-degreed teacher. • Sites would need to hold City of Arborville accreditation, and/or hold NAFCC accreditation. • Funds could be contracted on a per-child basis, so sites could serve any number of eligible 4-year-olds.

Reprinted with permission from Elsevier Press, 2005.

Public School Staff/ School Site	Public School Staff/ Community Site	Contracted Services/ Community Site	Contracted Services/Family Child-Care Home Site
Option IB: Two or more district classrooms • Same criteria as above except that extended education and care programming provided by nondistrict staff contracted with accredited nondistrict early learning centers on school site	• ECC staff will be supported in working toward licensure. • Minimum of 437 hours of "instruction" time provided for each child—site would have flexibility in scheduling within the school year.	• The contracted per-child funding could be used by the site in whatever way the site administrator chooses (e.g., enhanced salaries for staff, operational expenses, etc.). • Minimum of 437 hours of "instruction" time provided for each child—site would have flexibility in scheduling.	• The contracted per-child funding could be used by the site in whatever way the site provider chooses (e.g., enhanced salaries for staff, operational expenses, etc.). • Minimum of 437 hours of "instruction" time provided for each child—site would have flexibility in scheduling.
Option IC: One Classroom and child-care community site • AM and PM classes (2.5 hours each, school year) provided by district staff children enrolled based on: living in school combined attendance area, parents work in combined attendance area, other. Extended education and care programming provided by an accredited community agency (center-based or family home child-care offsite).	• Site could serve children from outside of ASD, but only ASD children would be funded. • ASD support services would follow the children. • Collaboration team comprises all partners to create appropriate match of teacher to center.	• Site could provide the program for children in a multi-aged group and serve children from outside of ASD, getting funding only for 4-year-old ASD children. • ASD support services would follow the children. • Collaborative team comprises all partners.	• Site could provide the program for children in a multi-aged group and serve children from outside of ASD, getting funding only for 4-year-old ASD children. • ASD support services would follow the children. • Collaborative team comprises all partners.

Although the primary reason for putting this preschool initiative on hold was financial, paradoxically, concerns were raised regarding the ECC composition and efforts. The ECC was not deemed to be representative of the community of early childhood providers and families of Arborville.

Participation in the ECC

Ball (1994) suggests that policy "discourse is about what can be said, and thought, and also about who can speak, when, where, and with what authority" (p. 21). According to Ball, the power in discourse is in the authority it gains through key actors and their social relationships in the policy process. Individuals continue to impact policy through their presence or absence and their adherence or defiance in each stage of the process. Who facilitated the meetings, who was invited to the meetings, and who spoke all provide insights into the power relationships at work in the ECC.

After the announcement that preschool for "at-risk" children in the district would end in the spring of 2001, a follow-up letter was sent from the district consultants to invite directors ("early childhood community members") to a summer workshop. How this initial mailing list was constructed and who constructed it raises issues of access and presence. A local nonprofit clearinghouse in conjunction with the ASD consultants generated the letter. Facilities included on the list were city accredited or were registered with a support organization for family child-care providers. Once the ECC was under way, the question of whom to contact was referred to as the "mailing list," the "council list," or the "team list." The ECC contact persons/mailing list comprised 297 recipients: 151 child-care/preschool community members (teachers, staff, and directors), 84 agency members (nonprofit clearinghouse, Arborville Head Start, State Council for Children and Families), 42 parents (as indicated by no agency/school affiliation), and 20 ASD personnel.

The names that later appeared as participants and committee members in the ECC represented the same population that had been involved in other related community committees (Literacy Campaign, etc.). For example, one of the initial consultants on the project also worked for Head Start and eventually became a collaborative writer for the state's education department and university representatives at the state economic summit in support of early childhood. She also worked with the Department of Education on projects regarding teacher licensure. In addition, three of the five key agency administrators had already worked on at least two other community committees together. Although it makes sense that interests overlap, the point is that the networks were fairly well established, and involvement on projects was based on prior experience on similar projects or recommendations of colleagues. The same leaders were involved in this process as were involved in other initiatives for children. The initial invitations were based on broad affiliation with early childhood education in the community. This suggests that district employees must have been familiar with either an individual or the agency to ensure an invitation.

Although just over half of the participants were individuals working in community child-care programs, only those in accredited centers were invited to the table. This meant that families of children attending nonaccredited child-care services—whether center- or home-based—had little representation on the ECC. The minutes of the October meeting indicated discussion regarding the failure to connect with nonaccredited centers and the lack of access to communities that might benefit the most from universal access. However, this concern, while officially documented, was not sufficiently important to secure next steps. No known additional outreach occurred with persons or groups that never made the original list.

Belonging to some kind of early childhood network played a large part in getting an invitation. These networks provided social capital (Bourdieu, 1984), as the power needed to access the ECC was available only to those belonging to these networks (accredited early childhood centers and recognized agencies).

TERMINOLOGY TIPS

Social capital refers to the "sum of the resources, actual or virtual, that accrue to an individual or a group by virtue of possessing a durable network of more or less institutionalized relationships of mutual acquaintance and recognition" (Bourdieu & Wacquant, 1992, p. 119). In other words, social networks carry value.

Attendance Requirements

An invitation was not necessarily a guarantee that individuals would be able to voice their perspectives and participate fully in the ECC. For example, take this vignette of a telephone call to Carol, a family child-care provider, during the second year of the ECC offers insight:

> *Carol:* Yeah, hi, can you hang on just a sec ... kids, keep it down. . . . Josh, please wait to pour your milk until I can help. Sorry, anyway, where is this meeting tomorrow? The research park? Where the heck is that? Is it on a bus line? If not, I just can't make it. It is—great. Okay, so I guess I'll see you tomorrow night.
>
> *Researcher:* It's at 7:30 A.M.
>
> *Carol:* What?! It's at 7:30 in the morning? There is *no* way I can make that—who would watch the kids? I can't just take off! This is crazy ... not only did I just hear about this yesterday through the grapevine but it is next to impossible for me to make it. It seems to me like they just don't want "my type" [family home care] there. I know it's not your fault ... but this whole idea of including the "community" seems bogus to me. Don't call yourself a collaboration if some of us who really care can't even participate.

As this conversation indicates, in order to participate at meetings, one must be available during the day, have child care available, have time for the project, speak English, and have transportation. While the meetings were located in a variety of sites (accredited child-care centers, Head Start, sponsoring agencies, etc.), little attention was given to the resources needed to enable individuals like Carol to attend. At the same time, some areas of town were not included as potential sites for meetings of the ECC. There were no southside centers represented in the collaboration other than Head Start, yet services and individuals in this area of Arborville served the highest proportion of families with lower resources. Given these conditions, the ECC comprised predominantly White middle-class women working in early childhood agencies who were provided with release time.

Analysis of meeting attendance indicates that a little over a year after the inception of the ECC, the majority (77%) of the participants were no longer providers of early childhood services, but administrative agency members and district employees. This may be a natural progression and unintentional. As mentioned previously, in order to get invited to the table and participate in the ECC, one had to have a certain amount of symbolic capital (social, economic, and cultural resources) or at least perceived capital (Bourdieu, 1977).

This capital was obtained by either belonging to an officially recognized agency or network concerned with early childhood education or working in a service deemed to be of a higher quality than others (e.g., accredited centers versus nonaccredited programs, center-based versus family home care). Individuals with symbolic capital have more power and authority than others and therefore tend to protect what they have. This capital enabled those involved in the ECC to use what Bourdieu (1984) calls symbolic violence.

In this situation, the notion of collaboration was used to disguise the invisible ways recognized early childhood agencies and individuals exercised power (invitation lists, district staff as facilitators) to protect their own interests. While the use of community collaboration implies inclusion, the agencies and individuals with more authority used their capital, perhaps unconsciously, to initially exclude nonaccredited centers, family child-care providers, and families in lower-resourced communities from policy formulation. This limited the participants constituting the ECC and "symbolically silenced" a large and diverse group of collaborators. Yet, this group of nonparticipants was the population that would most benefit from Universal Preschool. Given the invisible ways power was operating in the ECC, even if these marginalized groups were included at the policy table, could their voices be heard?

TERMINOLOGY TIPS

Symbolic capital is "the form that the various species of capital assume when they are perceived and recognized as legitimate" (Bourdieu, 1989, p. 17; see also Bourdieu, 1986). Simply put, symbolic capital is capital whose forms (economic, social, and cultural) are seen as valid.

TERMINOLOGY TIPS

Bourdieu introduces *symbolic violence* as a "censored" way in which power is used over others. This symbolic violence is a way of creating "relations of personal dependence" (veiled as either a gift or debt) without using overt economic or physical violence. Symbolic violence is used to further set up relations of domination or power differential (Bourdieu, 2000; Bourdieu & Wacquant, 1992).

Form and Structure of ECC Meetings and Forums

The following exchange took place at a November community forum created to inform the public regarding the work of the ECC:

> *Community member:* I have a question: Why haven't parents of young children been involved from the start?
> *Chairperson:* That is a great question, but we are out of time, I am sorry. I want to be respectful of people's personal time and we said we would wrap up promptly at 8:00. Thanks so much for coming.

In addition to who was invited to participate in the ECC, the structure of the collaboration changed over time, as evidenced in alterations to the meeting purpose and structure, room organization, and leadership. As exemplified in this conversation, the meeting structure changed from a rather open and "organic" process to one more highly structured and formal marked by strict time-keeping.

Meeting Structure

Initial forums, although guided, were open-ended and ambiguous. Framed as a journey, the purpose of these forums was to share information about the creation of a new Universal Preschool program and to seek the input of community members. The room arrangement invited participation as tables and chairs were arranged in small clusters to facilitate conversation and discussion of the issues (see Figure 3.2).

A year later, the purpose of the forum had not changed drastically. However, while the organizers still sought to build consensus and to share information about preschool policy, the room was not arranged to invite participation.

TERMINOLOGY TIPS

Unconscious bias (or *implicit bias*) often is defined as prejudice or unsupported judgments in favor of or against one thing, person, or group as compared with another, in a way that usually is considered unfair (www.vanderbilt.edu/diversity/unconscious-bias/).

Under new leadership, the public forum in August highlighted a PowerPoint presentation sharing facts about child-care centers, the district, and the number of children to be served. Some time was allowed for questions, but the room was set up in a lecture style so that participation and discussion among all individuals present was curtailed (see Figure 3.3).

Finally, at the ASD board meeting, the board viewed the process and the presentation literally from the center of the room (see Figure 3.4). In that position, the board members could be perceived as holding the power to support or veto. Although the process was marketed as democratic in nature, with time set aside for public input, it quickly became obvious that phone calls were made to individual board members by concerned residents to better ensure that their voices were heard through a position of perceived power. This supports the notion that there were community members willing to be involved, who had been overlooked at some point, and who now recognized the opportunity to get involved through the elected officials at the table.

These images illustrate how the contexts of the meetings shifted from encouraging interaction, to a presentation-style setting, to the board room. The shift from a more abstract gathering to efficient meetings was not necessarily contradictory to collaboration, but many times efficiency trumped voice. As the form and structure of the meetings changed, individual power was even less likely: Voices were constrained to specific time frames within an agenda, often determined by outside agencies, particularly the ASD, rather than members of the ECC.

Figure 3.2. Meeting Structure A

Figure 3.3. Meeting Structure B

Figure 3.4. Meeting Structure C

A False Sense of Power

Foucault (1980) suggests that there is a false sense of power in governance structures such as board meetings or public forums. For Foucault, power does not reside in a person, group, movement, or artifact, but instead circulates through social relations:

Power is employed and exercised through a net-like organization. And not only do individuals circulate between its threads; they are always in the position of simultaneously undergoing and exercising this power. They are not only its inert or consenting target; they are always also the elements of its articulation. In other words, individuals are the vehicles of power, not its points of application. (p. 98)

Therefore, the issue of who gets to be at the table and participate in the collaborative is the wrong question. Rather, by recognizing policy as both text and discourse, the issue becomes not so much the power of voice, but rather the power relations attached to the voice.

For the ECC, the authority for policy implementation resided with the ASD and its board of education. It was the board that tabled implementing the policy, claiming an inadequacy of resources, only to announce 3 months later the creation of a new partnership with the research center at the university and Head Start to implement a pilot preschool program at Greentree Elementary beginning in September. Despite the creation of the ECC, and efforts made to include diverse voices of the community, the ECC policy process began with the ASD board.

As one Head Start administrator said:

... we [the ECC group] are not in charge, so you can't be completely collaborative. But there's been a lot of collaboration in setting up the model and trying to figure out how they'll [district and child-care providers] work together ... it's a collaboration as much as it can be when you have a single decisionmaker [ASD] but you know that, that's still not bad. ... Yeah, the only true collaboration would be everybody puts in a portion and there is a consensus building and that's pretty much utopia.

Recognizing that the goals for the initiative may be shared but are initiated by the district describes an *enacted partnership* that has been found to be more challenging when trying to reach satisfaction across participants (Seddon, Billett, & Clemans, 2005).

VOICES IN
CURRENT UNIVERSAL PRESCHOOL EFFORTS

How can we learn from past experiences to increase the diversity of voices at the table and acknowledge how power impacts community–partner relationships? Universal Preschool programs have seen a dramatic increase between 2002 (past) and 2019 (present). NIEER (2019) released the 16th edition of their annual report, *The State of Preschool 2018*, which tracks state-funded preschool access, resources, and quality. The report indicates growing disparities in enrollment, investments, and quality (Friedman-Krauss et al., 2019). Could this be partly a result of the voices of teachers, families, and the community not being heard, validated, and integrated into Universal Preschool policies?

The needs of children, families, and communities are complex and continually evolving. Some of the needs evident in 2019 include more services for dual-language learners, attention to families who may be experiencing homelessness, and programming complexities due to the opioid epidemic. The pressures on preschool teaching staff and administrators are growing, without the necessary compensation or resources to provide high-quality programming to meet these complex needs. Preschool programs are asked to involve families in the education of their children, without regard to the challenges of balancing parenting and life complexities.

What about the decisions that need to be made every day when in a Universal Preschool collaboration? Many collaborations already exist, so the nuances of participation and perspectives lie in the details of everyday planning and programming (Barnett, Robin, et al., 2003; Schulman & Blank, 2009). Those making decisions at the policy level may not have a realistic view of the challenges of implementing Universal Preschool services. This may result in ineffective or confusing requirements for staff members and families. In existing programs, who is included and how they are understood remain an issue. Family Fun Nights at many Head Start sites are structured to bring together staff, family, and children. In the "Present" story below, a district representative visits a Family Fun Night, and the issue of waning family attendance is observed and questioned. With the luxury of reading back through the interactions, one is able to recognize how this absence is understandable.

FAMILY PERSPECTIVE

We think our child is learning many things at preschool and can see that the teacher works hard. They keep wanting us to come to school for meetings, but our work schedules change a lot. There is not always an interpreter there either, so it makes it hard to follow multiple and overlapping conversations.

PRESENT STORY: I DON'T KNOW WHY THEY DON'T COME

Kristin Whyte

It's about 5:10 P.M. and the first family presses the buzzer to be let in the building for Family Fun Night. Laura, a Head Start pre-K teacher, lets them in. This event happens once a month. Families trickle in and by 5:35 six families are there. They go through the motions of a familiar event—these are the same six families who typically come. They have dinner, then head downstairs to the classroom to do a picture-drawing and writing activity together, which Laura runs. Afterward, the children stay downstairs with the support staff while Laura, the family outreach worker, and most of the parents head upstairs for a Parent Advisory Council (PAC) meeting.

This particular day, a woman from the local district was there to talk to the families about kindergarten expectations. Along with tips for activities to do with their children, she kept telling the families how important they are: "You're important; you're their first teacher; no one can take that away from you." These compliments, assertions, and tips are accompanied by "buts": " . . . but we need you to work as a team"; "I know parents are busy, but . . . " The families and Laura sat and listened while the family outreach worker translated into Spanish. On occasion, Laura nodded when the district worker emphasized activities that she said promote school readiness.

Not all PAC meetings are as formal or as quiet. For instance, most of the same families attended a meeting about pre-K graduation, but the tone was entirely different. Conversation between the families and Laura flowed as they collaboratively planned the event. Laura came with ideas, and the families also offered up their own thoughts. Then, both the teacher and the families came to the (very well-attended) graduation at the end of the school year.

While almost all of the families came to pre-K graduation, it was disappointing to Laura that not many attended the other Family Fun Nights. While cleaning up after one such night, in a moment of disappointment, she exclaimed, "I don't know why they don't come. I know people are working, but we have fun. It's not boring. And we always provide dinner and child care." Although frustrated, Laura also expressed that she knew that families cared about their children and valued their children's education; they just had so much going on in their lives that it was easy to overlook participating in school activities.

SUMMARY

The ways in which participants—whether family members, teachers, or district staff—are invited, recognized, and addressed matters in terms of building collaboration among diverse populations. In the 2016 NIEER *State of Preschool Yearbook*, findings indicate that resources and support systems for

— Ref. b/tw two arrows in #5..

dual-language learners fall short (Barnett et al., 2017). In this "Present" story, a translator was present, yet were there other linguistic and cultural barriers, created by the dominant discourses and notions of family participation, that caused misunderstandings or misinterpretations? Research suggests the need to consider different ways of engaging with diverse family strengths (González, Moll, & Amanti, 2005; Whyte & Karabon, 2016). How educators perceive families through relationships of power and position impacts how the universal aspect of a preschool policy is implemented at the program-site level.

Individuals need capital in order to access and participate with authority in policy discourses. Collaboration provides one way to build social capital (Chrislip, 2002). To ensure broader participation in early childhood policy initiatives, those who already have access to networks and authority must make every effort to consider who is involved. Those with access are in a position to enable community members to participate in policy formulation. One simple way to enable broader participation is to hold meetings across the community, at a variety of times and places, as well as providing child care so that all those with responsibilities for young children can attend. Providing food creates not only a convenience for families, but also a powerful

suggestions for equitable policy making vs. teachers

Entering New Territory

societal connection. Through the sharing of food, conversation becomes a bit less formal and a broader sense of perspective sharing is fostered. Similarly, invitations need to go out to agencies and individuals that are usually not accessible via typical networks. This may mean canvassing the neighborhood and building a potential mailing list from the ground up. Such efforts will ensure broader participation at the beginning of an initiative. Seeking out leaders in a variety of settings (church, school, community) brings in a variety of cultural capital and builds access to specific communities within the district.

Once broader participation is achieved, it is necessary to consider ways of providing social capital to those often excluded from the policy table (families, nonaccredited programs, for-profit child care) so that their perspectives are included in the decisionmaking process. This is a much larger task fraught with complexity, given the differing discourses and power relations that shape policymaking. One way this social capital might be accrued is through the creation of counternarratives to dominant understandings of what it means to be able to speak for early childhood (Ryan & Grieshaber, 2004). Discourses have power only because individuals speak and write them into existence; therefore, one way these counternarratives gain credence is through the building of alliances. The ECC, for example, helped motivate child-care teachers and agencies to band together, thereby increasing the power they had in the policymaking process. Perhaps temporarily, this small group "wrote" its story as powerful by banding together and presenting at the board meeting. This allowed for input as a collective voice of early childhood educators and families at the district level, although, as noted throughout this chapter, power was limited and key voices were missing from the table.

Finally, if these counternarratives are to have continued presence and force in the field, it is crucial that those working in early childhood document their efforts. Much of the work on early childhood policy is written from an academic or economic perspective. Research evidence is used to bolster economic arguments for the benefits of an early education. Silin and Lippman (2003) provide one example of this type of documentation work in which teachers, staff developers, and administrators working in an urban setting write about their experiences in a policy collaboration process.

If early childhood policy is to be responsive to the communities in which it is enacted, then collaboration must be redefined as a policy goal. Instead of bringing together communities on the pretense of eliciting their perspectives, efforts must be made to develop the social capital of marginalized groups and document local efforts to make change. In addition, keen attention to the nature of the partnership is needed. Is this a negotiable collaborative effort with reciprocal goals for all stakeholders (Seddon, Billett, and Clemans, 2005)? While there is no "one way" to create preschool policy, by acknowledging the politics and power of the process, it may be possible to develop programs that meet the needs of those they serve.

REFLECTIVE CONVERSATIONS AND ACTIONS

1. Consider the theory and criteria from the "Past" story. Power differentials exist and change in context but all circulate within a dominant discourse as it connects to our nation, culture (geographic, racial, ethnic, economic), and subculture (ECE). Add in the ideas of the construction of inclusion (meeting structure, attendance) and consider ongoing practice—forms and how they are communicated, participation in events when there are other pressures, and the need to connect across lines of power. Finally, consider that public schools and early care and education often operate on different schedules. Based on the above, answer the following:
   - How could collaboration meetings be structured to include everyone?
   - How could technology be used to obtain input from a wide variety of stakeholders even if they are unable to attend meetings in person?

2. Consider the idea of symbolic capital and networks from the "Past" story. What are some reasons families aren't able to attend the Family Fun Nights as outlined in the "Present" story—both the obvious and the less obvious power-related reasons? What differences do you notice in approaches to include all families between the "Past" and "Present" stories?

3. Using factors from the "Past" story, what might contribute to Laura's understanding of family in the "Present" story? The social position of the family? How are family members defined? What pressures might Laura be feeling? What pieces were in place to support families? What assumptions have been made about family involvement and how might policy and center programming address these assumptions? Cite examples at the personal, programmatic, community, and federal levels.

4. Think of a time you participated in a voluntary community event (dorm meeting, orientation, neighborhood association). Now think of a mandatory event (orientation session, staff meeting, etc.). What were the differences in terms of feeling either connected or alienated? Why? What relationships were in place to make the meeting successful? What were some of the barriers to deeper communication? How does this connect with models of collaboration as enacted or negotiated?

5. What types of strategies and activities could be used to make community or other meetings more interactive? Why is asking "who gets to sit at the table" the wrong question, and how does this impact inclusion and interaction? — Is this the wrong question?

6. How might insights from this chapter inform current initiatives, such as Power to the Profession (mentioned in Chapter 1), to include all voices in the field? What forms of capital may be missing for inclusion? What networks could be used to create a stronger message to support ECE professionals?

CHAPTER 4

Equitable Access to Universal Preschool

Enrollment Issues

The intent of universal access to public preschool programs and services may be thwarted when policy decisions do not account for placements in the best interests of children and families. These policy decisions, while seemingly benign, can evolve into actions that may reinforce multiple forms of segregation. Who decides which families will receive preschool services and in which locations? Herein are underlying issues of power and perspective for universal access.

POLICY IS MULTIFACETED

Policy does not happen in isolation; it exists within the currents of power and knowledge, influenced by the roles that race, ability, language, and class play. Critical race theory is one way to analyze access to Universal Preschool. CRT was created out of a legal movement (Critical Legal Studies) and considers the "relationship among race, racism and power" and places them in the context of "economics, history, context, group- and self-interest, and even feelings and the unconscious" (Delgado & Stefancic, 2001, pp. 2–3).

Specifically, within CRT the notion of interest convergence is a helpful tool to describe how discordant social movements converge to serve the "greater good" (Bell, 1987). Interest convergence suggests that when the interests of the dominant (White) culture and the interests of the nondominant (Black, Latinx, Indigenous, etc.) culture converge on an issue (e.g., desegregating schools), political change occurs. However, many times movements that seemingly address the desires of both groups indeed end up continuing to serve the needs of the dominant group. In other words, even though a variety of stakeholders may start with a common goal, as the process shifts over time, not all stakeholders stand to benefit equally.

Could Universal Preschool initiatives perpetuate older educational models that historically have provided unequal access to children and families based on their socioeconomic status, geographic location, or racial background?

> **TERMINOLOGY TIPS**
>
> *Interest convergence* suggests that when the interests of the dominant culture and the interests of the nondominant culture converge on an issue, political change occurs yet continues to serve the interests of the dominant culture.

Who is making the enrollment decisions that affect the lives of these young children and their families?

As outlined in Chapter 2, implementing a collaborative Universal Preschool approach brings with it various federal, state, local, and agency standards, policies, funding, and other requirements. Individual agencies may have requirements to serve a certain percentage of children with special needs, or bus routes may impact attendance decisions. The continued story of one pilot program provides perspective on the complexity of creating and orchestrating universal access.

PAST STORY: ECC—COME ONE, COME ALL

Hector bounds across the Greentree Elementary School cafeteria (in late August) smiling at his younger sister. "Esta es mi escuela!" He flashes a smile so big, it can hardly contain his joy. Hector is 4 years old and has just proclaimed Greentree as "his" school. However, because his family meets the income requirements for Head Start, administrators instead enroll him at Waterfront Head Start (starting in September). Ironically, a Spanish-speaking teacher is available only at the Greentree site where Hector will no longer attend.

The experience of Hector and his family illustrates unintended consequences in Universal Preschool enrollment policies and in the interpretation and implementation of those policies. His story shines light into a corner of the policy "room" and illuminates why policy, while well meaning, is never perfect and, as Ball (1994) suggests, is "never closed, never complete." Policy as intended and written can look very different when enacted. Morphing of policy has potential for changes in outcomes at every step of the process.

This fluid nature of policy is "dangerous" (Rabinow, 1984, p. 343) as it signals opportunity to acknowledge larger social movements or discourses at play. Illuminating discourses such as universal access opens the opportunity to change the direction of policy. This "shift" acknowledges how global and concrete policy (enrollment for Universal Preschool, in this case), when enacted, is neither globally applicable nor concrete.

Part of this discussion revolves around the impact discourse has on collaborative decisionmaking. What do we mean by discourse? As defined in Chapter 2, it is a dynamic that constructs certain meanings around a topic or group

TERMINOLOGY TIPS

Policy, as defined by Stephen Ball (1994), is text that is read and interpreted and is the "product of compromises at various stages" of policy development, negotiation, and interpretation (p. 16).

(Foucault, 1972). For example, universal access suggests that all children have equal access to comparable programs. However, when this is examined closely, it is a more complicated idea. While the term *universal access* has been crafted through discourse to carry particular meanings (equitable access), the truth in the term may or may not exist depending on experience.

SCHOOL DISTRICT SPECIAL EDUCATION DIRECTOR PERSPECTIVE

We are required to provide special education services for all 3- and 4-year-old children who are eligible, in the least restrictive environment. Our district offers a program only for 4-year-olds, so we struggle to figure out how to provide services to the 3-year-olds. Some local early childhood providers are fearful of enrolling children with disabilities, and we have not developed the itinerant services to support these providers. Some families are asked to bring their 3-year-old child to the school for speech therapy, and many have complained about inconvenience due to work schedules and other complications. We are exploring a collaborative Universal Preschool program for 3- and 4-year-olds. Early education providers and families all seem excited about the possibility.

ENROLLMENT DECISIONS

As we follow Hector through his UPK experience, we discover that he may not have been placed in the most appropriate setting to nurture his growth and development. Hector was sharing his newfound joy in school in late August at the Greentree public school site. The pilot program was registering and enrolling children for a program that started in early September. For Hector, this meant changing "his" school to the Waterfront Head Start site.

How did the discussion and planning regarding enrollment fail and lead to his confusing and sudden move to the Head Start site? During the first year of the pilot, enrollment decisions often were made at the last minute, and while this accommodated some programming needs, it did not always work in favor of the child (and family).

Enrollment was an area of concern that was raised in administrative meetings throughout the year; this brought to light the confusion about classroom composition as well as policy requirements for the pilot program. In the planning stages of the pilot, it was decided that enrollment would be capped at 19

TERMINOLOGY TIPS

Bilingual education (BLE) is a program in which two languages are used to provide content matter instruction.

Biliteracy (BLL) is the ability to effectively communicate or understand written thoughts and ideas through the grammatical systems, vocabularies, and written symbols of two different languages.

Dual-language learner (DLL) is a child who is learning a second language while continuing to develop the home language.

Dual-language program/Dual immersion or *two-way immersion* or *two-way bilingual education* describes instruction designed to serve both language-minority and language-majority students concurrently.

Early childhood English language learner (ECELL) is a child between the ages of zero and 5 (early stages of development) who is in the process of learning English as a Second Language.

English language learners (ELLs) are students who are in the process of learning English.

Heritage languages are generally minority languages in society and typically are learned at home during childhood.

English as a Second Language (ESL) is a program of techniques, methodology, and special curriculum designed to teach ELL students English-language skills, which may include listening, speaking, reading, writing, study skills, content vocabulary, and cultural orientation.

Adapted from: www.colorincolorado.org/ell-basics/ell-glossary

children per section, and approximately 40% (or seven children in each section) would be identified as English language learners (ELLs), students with special needs, or both.

Figure 4.1 indicates the approximate classroom composition for the first year of the UPK pilot (there were transitions in and out of both programs as the year progressed):

In this pilot, identifying only certain characteristics of students in the planning policy phase led to real consequences for children and families. The racial/ethnic breakdown of students—beyond first language and special needs—was not included, as it was not stated as a factor in the original goals. Looking at this example, how do we provide for the best interests of all children without engaging in unintended discrimination or segregation? Identity markers such as ability, race, language, and class are at times conflated, particularly when working with policies that promote concepts such as universal access. For example, in the Arborville School District, a plan was put in place to help address the overrepresentation of certain ethnic groups in special education. The following was mentioned in a report from 2006: "Put directly, to be an African American or a Native American student in the Arborville school district means you are twice as likely to be in special education as a white student."

Figure 4.1. Classroom Composition

	CLASSROOM		
	Greentree A.M.	Greentree P.M.	Head Start
Enrollment Goals	19	19	19
Actual Enrollment	15	16	16
Composition Goals: 40% Special Needs and/or ELL	7	7	7
Actual Number of Children Enrolled with Special Needs and Children Who Are ELLs	2 (13%)	5 (31%)	5 (31%)
Actual Number of Children Enrolled Who Are ELLs	0	2	4

Note: Data taken from classroom fieldnotes October 13, 2003, and November 10, 2003, and do not account for dual placement (special needs and ELL).

This conflation of race and ability suggests the need to consider race as a social construction, particularly in relation to universal policies (Haney-Lopez, 1997). Racial diversity was implied through quantifying the goals for ELL and special education students in this pilot program. While the goal was to enroll approximately 40% of children who were ELL or had special needs, the first-year percentages were 13% and 31%, respectively, at Greentree and 0% and 31%, respectively, at Head Start (the teacher at Head Start was an English-only speaker). Ironically, the only bilingual teacher had only two ELLs out of 31 students for the first year, while the English-only teacher had four. The original enrollment plan and the actual numbers of children obviously varied. Did this happen because there were no Spanish-speaking families in the Greentree attendance area? Was it because Head Start had strict enrollment policies of its own? Or was it more complicated? Although these numbers may seem minimal, it is helpful to explore this phenomenon using critical analysis. Use of this analysis provides a cautionary tale and lends insights for future collaborations.

Implications of Federal, State, and Local Policies

Because this pilot included Head Start, federal policy had a major impact on local interpretations of collaborative policy. At the time, existing federal Head Start policies were followed for class size (minimum of 18), income requirements (100% of poverty threshold), and age requirements (3–5 mixed-age versus 4-year-olds only). Head Start administrators felt great pressure to fill their classrooms with at least 18 children, while the public school did not have the same pressure (at least initially). This is one example of how Head Start appeared to have less autonomy (due to federal policy) in contrast to the district program. The administrators' literal interpretation of the policy (the classes must be filled) exerted power over others (the pilot and classroom teachers).

The pressure to fill the Head Start classroom was expressed in the following interview with Pam Gallagher, a Head Start teacher:

> [Head Start enrollment policy] was harder for me to understand because being in the UPK program, when we were first enrolling and I wasn't up to 18 kids, they [Head Start administrators] were . . . a little bit hard on Adriane, the family outreach worker, and myself for not having our class size up. In my opinion, it was hard because you already had the income level which was . . . one thing they [families] had to meet. They already had to be 4 years old going into kindergarten and then you had the parameter that they had to be on a bus route . . . you want us to have this many kids but you have all these stipulations that we have to follow. . . . It's not that I don't agree with their policy. I just found it really difficult to follow.

Pam shared that the classroom minimum requirement caused the administrators to put pressure on the teachers and that she found it difficult to adhere to this particular policy. Along with the novelty of the pilot and the start of a new year, the pressure was apparent to "fill the class." Although the numbers were low at both sites the first year, this Head Start teacher continued to be given new students throughout the year. There was federal Head Start policy regarding optimum class size; however, individual agencies interpreted this policy differently, and some took the threat of closure very seriously. The enrollment parameters were not explicitly tied to race, rather, they were based on socioeconomic status. However, the 2000 Arborville census data revealed that in this district lower-resourced areas were populated by a much higher percentage of children and families of color. Therefore, at a federal level, the policy skewed the local enrollment using existing program policy. Based on Head Start policy requirements at the time, it appeared that the Waterfront Head Start site would enroll more children of color than the Greentree public site. In addition to the influence of federal policy, staff interpretation of the pilot policy complicated universal notions of access through the issue of "turf."

Turf Issues

> Yeah. Well the motivation is control, and they [district administrators] just can't fathom, they can't get their heads around the idea that another group could take leadership in a significant district. They say things like 'those would be our 4-year-olds' (Deborah Wells, director of outreach services).

Whose Turf

The director of outreach services highlighted the issue of who will provide educational programming for the 4-year-olds of this community. This administrator held a unique position in this pilot as she had clout through her affiliation with city offices and over 30 years of service to the early childhood education community. She suggested that the school district might fear that as child-care centers enrolled more students for Universal Preschool, centers would gain too much leadership power in the education of young children. She further suggested that the issue of enrollment stemmed from program control issues. Specifically, the district was afraid of losing control and therefore "claimed" the children. However, it was also apparent that each agency (Head Start, the district, and child-care centers) strove to "keep" the children they had, out of fear of losing income and subsequently their programs. The administrator implied that during negotiations for the collaboration, the need to "claim" children as numbers for enrollment to justify continued financial support was prioritized. In the politically marginalized world of early education, this fear of lost income is understandable.

> In the pilot, the first-year enrollment was a mess. This year, it went very well. They [district administrators] were very responsive to leaving our enrollees alone but the first year they didn't have a lot of kids. They want us ... to serve the most needy, who we are already serving. UPK has to serve anybody so we sort of ended up with a skewed population. We had ours [students] but the first year they really took a number, several of ours, and

it was hard to fill them in and that will continue to be a problem as this is implemented regardless of where it is because there will be some parents that say—especially low-income parents and people that have very little resources—I'm going to go where it's free. Anything that's going to save me the money, and that results in inconsistencies for children, which we know we don't want. (Head Start director, Arborville)

As the Head Start director recounts her frustration regarding the enrollment of children, there is a strong sense of ownership through her use of the word *ours* to refer to students who normally would enroll in Head Start. While there is an issue of "turf" at play in the enrollment process, some who are involved are trying to balance the need to fill the program (federal influence on Head Start) with the need to create an equitable program for all children.

These examples and perspectives highlight the paradoxical discourses at play. One discourse is about Head Start being business savvy (to fill the classes), another is the discourse too often attached to targeted or compensatory programs (low-income children need a "Head Start"), and still another is about offering access to all children (equitable programming for all) (Beatty, 2012). How can we move beyond the inherent debate among these discourses to find the connecting thread and determine what is possible?

Although clear enrollment goals expressed as percentages were created for the pilot, the planning and implementation of collaborative policies around enrollment were complicated because multiple agencies were involved. The desire to "do the right thing" for children became confusing. The issues of filling classes to keep a program alive or funded, and meeting individual needs (such as Hector's), became real dilemmas in the definition, planning, and implementation of access.

Using the critical race theory tenet of interest convergence, we ask, whose interest was served when making enrollment decisions? In this case, there were many answers: Head Start needed to meet enrollment minimums, the school district had to address transportation needs, and initial organizers needed clear policy to justify enrollment decisions. In the end, were Hector's needs met? With Spanish as his home language, he was placed with an English-only teacher rather than with a fluent Spanish-speaking teacher at another site. While the universal nature of the policy (all interested children were enrolled in the UPK program) seemed intact, the interests of the agencies were prioritized over those of the child whose first language was Spanish.

Location, Location, Location

"We have all had the experience of finding that our reactions and perhaps even our deeds have denied beliefs we thought were ours."

—James Baldwin, 1956/2011

This quote relates to the internal struggle that many participants expressed in terms of working to meet the needs of all children through the broad policy of universal access. While well intentioned, some reactions to the process of enrollment reinforced ideas of racial and class segregation. The program began with a pilot that consisted of only three classrooms. Even within this small pilot, the complicated issue of writing enrollment policy surfaced. As concurrent discussions were held on the bigger picture of rolling out the pilot program for all children in the district, this enrollment policy continued to be an issue.

During the policy formulation stage (Rist, 1998), conversations included exploration of the ability of existing early childhood centers to enroll and transport children. At least initially, it appeared that, in the name of reducing transitions, accredited private early childhood programs would continue to serve the children currently enrolled.

Accreditation in the early education environment refers to a process of meeting requirements that exceed state child-care licensing standards. However, the geographic areas that were lacking accredited child-care centers were lower-resource areas, which meant the children in these areas would either be bussed or attend public school sites in their neighborhood. This did not necessarily mean a difference in services or quality, but it is important to recognize this as a separation of sorts (by program type and socioeconomic status). This is similar to the de facto segregation many of the nation's public schools continue to face (Mervosh, 2019). In other words, while community interests can converge around reducing transitions for children (e.g., not bussing), the policy becomes one of racial segregation.

> If I could create it in a perfect world, all children in the City of Arborville—no matter what socioeconomic background, race—[all] children and families would have convenient, accessible, multicultural, inclusive programming for educational, social, emotional, high-family-involvement programming with wrap-around care services in neighborhoods that they live in. So they'd see their friends, so parents at the end of a work day or nonwork day could come and pick them up, and they wouldn't have to sit in the car for 45 minutes or they'd have a very short bus ride home. So kids, young children, would have as few transitions as possible in a nurturing, caring atmosphere. . . . It's just specifically designed for 4-year-olds, nested in a neighborhood with certified teachers. (Nancy Peters, lead elementary principal)

ideal

Nancy remains optimistic as she continues to describe the attendance situation geographically:

> I think the chances of realizing [that] . . . are good because when I look at a map of the City of Arborville and see where the providers are located . . .

and where the space in the schools is available . . . I think [it's] geographically doable. (Nancy Peters, lead elementary principal)

However, when it gets down to what access means in real terms, the population is segregated.

> We're talking about accredited centers. . . . Not in high-poverty neighborhoods, but what exists is school space. . . . If you have accredited centers in higher-income areas, there's usually not school space available. So you really do need to depend on one another [community child care and the school district]. I mean, this isn't going to work unless we work together. (Nancy Peters, lead elementary principal)

Based on the existing geographic layout that this principal described, children with fewer economic resources would be in public school sites, and children in middle- to higher-income homes would be in private sites with public programs. Although Nancy described program segregation, public versus private, she also acknowledged the need to depend on one another. This suggests the potential for conversation among community members. Deborah, the director of outreach services, explains her understanding of the geography and enrollment in terms of accreditation and quality.

> There are a couple of religious programs . . . and some of the for-profits, depending on the day of the week and staff that are there, it's less than custodial because they run the staff through there so fast. They'll operate without enough staff and then they pay their fines; they're making money. And the lower-income kids, a lot of them, are concentrated in the worst-quality care. (Deborah Wells, Director of Outreach Services)

This perspective of an early childhood leader brings a sense of reality to the situation. A dilemma surfaced in terms of the precarious nature of financing. Is there an unintended consequence that children in lower-resource situations end up in nonaccredited (potentially low-quality) centers because most of the accredited centers are in higher-resource neighborhoods?

While Nancy maintained there was equality in public and private sites, Deborah suggested that perhaps one solution was to move centers that served higher-resource families into lower-resource areas.

> Another goal I had was for the city to help finance child care as part of a redevelopment grant and to provide not just space but an operating fund that will allow that center to serve low-income kids. I would like to see more economic integration of children. So I'd love to see the Creativity Center [a Reggio-based preschool] build a center in Pine Valley [a low-resource area] or the university [build there]. But you know, most likely it will be Head

Start, which is unfortunate. I appreciate their willingness to do it, but they're not going to draw high-income families in there, and that's when the kids really make gains in vocabulary and social skills is when they have those [higher-resourced families].

Integration through subsidies (as suggested by Deborah), sliding scales, or including children across ability levels (e.g., 3- to 5-year-old special education services) is seen as offering collaborative solutions toward inclusion; however, there are initiatives that show targeted programs as offering gains for students as well (Beatty, 2012; Fuller, 2014; Schweinhart & Weikart, 1997; Weiland & Yoshikawa, 2013). Telling this "Past" story brings to light a caution for how we define universal access. In searching for a solution for relevant and responsive education for all children, consideration of access through a variety of program designs and delivery models may serve individual needs more appropriately. In other words, while the term *universal* suggests access for all, there is still a risk of creating separate programming that may not be equitable. Perhaps it is less important *how* children access ECE and more important that they *have* access to relevant, equitable education. In other studies regarding Universal Preschool collaborative programming, enrollment issues rose to the surface as problematic, specifically in terms of serving populations with lower resources or those who are marginalized (Wilinski, 2017b). It is striking that the initial problems with Universal Preschool rollout continue to surface in more recent research studies.

PRESENT STORY: ENROLLMENT SILOS AND CONUNDRUMS

Sarah Galanter-Guziewski

As a principal of a public school with 4K, I see many benefits and struggles. Our program is located in the elementary school where I work as principal, in private preschools, and at a Head Start site.

Enrollment

Families enroll in 4K electronically. If they don't have online access, we have a date in the spring and an additional date in the fall for them to enroll. Some of the district elementary schools do not have space for 4K in their buildings, but all students can participate in 4K at a neighboring school. However, one glitch is that perhaps a student's house is in the assigned attendance area but the wrap-around care (before care and/or after care) is in another attendance area. In that event, the student cannot get transportation to the next site. At our school, we have community child-care agencies that will come and get students from our school and take them to the wrap-around care, and we have a preschool that happens to be in our attendance area that also provides wrap-around care. Our 4K program is only half days, 4 days a week. Due to this crazy schedule, many children are unable to enroll and come to kindergarten with no prior school experience. Head Start has a few spots in our area for students who need full-day care and who meet the income requirements.

Spanish–English Bilingual Students

At our school we have a kindergarten to 5th-grade bilingual program but it does not include 4K. Some students who come to us for 5K attended a bilingual 4K at Head Start. In actuality, it is the assistants who can speak Spanish and work with some small groups in Spanish, but the group times and head teacher–led times are in English. Some students who come to the school's 4K and have little English are enrolled in our English 4K. We have bilingual resource specialists who can help translate, but the educational language is English. Some of the children then go to our bilingual kindergartens and have some confusion regarding letter sounds, especially vowels.

The district has two sites with bilingual 4K but neither is at our building. This remains a big issue. We have 25 5-year-olds coming into our bilingual program; none of them have had 4K with a bilingual Spanish lead teacher and some have had no bilingual lessons at all.

Special Education

Students who are in Head Start or community programs and who have already been identified with special needs in 4K receive itinerant services through the school district. Students who are in the school-based 4K are part of our school's special education teacher's caseload. This deeper knowledge of the students in 4K within our school leads to more appropriate goals and services as the students enter kindergarten. Because the itinerant teachers don't know the school, we often have to change the IEPs as students enter 5K at our school. This means additional meetings for staff and parents, and sometimes the students do not get what they need right at the start of the school year.

Families

Head Start has an advantage over the school site due to its location being closer to the homes of the families enrolled. It also has community outreach workers who are readily available. This allows the staff to have a better understanding of the culture of the neighborhood, including the strengths and more general issues in the area. The ratio of family outreach workers to students is smaller, so the workers have an easier time doing home visits and connecting directly with the families. At the school there is only one social worker for 570 students.

One of the advantages of being at the school-based 4K classroom is that children often can be with their siblings and participate in the evening and daytime events at the school. We also can begin at younger ages to develop relationships between school staff and parents, which is helpful as the years go on. Our school has a nurse, a social worker, and a psychologist who can serve the 4K students in the school program.

[handwritten marginalia: Sees pros/cons of school vs. community 4K. Being in a school does not always mean continuity of teachers + programs]

Community

The 4K students who come to the school have the advantage of being part of the greater community. For example, 4K students go to assemblies; participate in our schoolwide behavior system; access library story time at the school; know staff members like the social worker, nurse, and psychologist; as well as attend concerts, book readings, and other events in upper-grade classrooms. Their transition into kindergarten—over the 7 years we have had preschool onsite—seems to be easier than that of students who had 4K at a community or Head Start site. For students who have participated in 4K at our school, there are very few behavior calls at the beginning of the year, and if there is a behavior issue, we likely have a plan in place already. For some students, being part of such a big school seems to be overwhelming, and our 4K in the school can ease them into the "big" school more smoothly.

Communication

[handwritten marginalia: — Principal's take on facilitating 4K + 5K transitions.]

There is a school district 4K department, and I am aware that it provides professional development to all 4K sites. However, as an administrator at a school site, I have very little communication with other sites that feed into our school (including Head Start). This is something I probably should pursue more, so that the incoming kindergartners could visit the 5K classrooms and the school or I could go talk to them about school. Each spring, I think I should do more to reach out, and then the school year starts up in fall and things get busy and I don't make it happen. I think that it is difficult for the Head Start teachers because their students attend so many different elementary schools in my district, as well as the surrounding districts, so it must be overwhelming to think of connecting with so many schools.

SUMMARY

"The paradox of education is precisely this—that as one begins to become conscious one begins to examine the society in which he [*sic*] is being educated."

—James Baldwin, 1963, p. 42

The more we look at solutions, the greater the need to consider the context in which we are solving the ECE problems. Given that the policy process is continually evolving (Ball, 1994), illuminating discourses such as universal access opens the opportunity to shift policy paths. The influence of agency enrollment policy interfered with meeting individual child needs. Head Start has a specific mandate to target populations to provide compensatory support. This, at times, can make collaboration a bit tricky. Issues of "control" fueled the need for each organization to retain students, as children were tied to funding streams. While the discourse of universal access (e.g., serving all children or socioeconomic integration) impacted stakeholders (the city and the district), it bordered on "dangerous" as there was potential for this social and political movement to evolve into actions that reinforced segregation and inequity in resources (Bell, 1987).

The policy as intended looked different. Deborah Wells suggested that children with lower resources would gain academically and socially by attending the same schools as children with higher resources. Leaders expressed a desire to create a better learning situation for all children. However, "dangerous" intersections in terms of interest convergence were uncovered. First, although there was recognition of separate services (e.g., accredited centers in neighborhoods with more resources), the solutions either continued to segregate public and private (at least initially) or fit into the deficit model in which the strengths of home communities are not recognized. While the initial policy of enrollment and universal access to enrollment was heralded as a progressive policy initiative, if this discourse is not questioned on multiple levels, it will indeed continue to segregate children and families.

There is continued evidence that compensatory education programs have lessened or are ameliorating the achievement gap in later school years (Beatty, 2012). In addition, many communities of color are asking for separate education options so they can build culturally authentic programs in which community members teach children within their own community (e.g., Harlem Children's Zone, Indigenous cultural and language immersion schools). Consideration of the historical legacy of separate but equal educational missteps is warranted. This is not just a question of economics but also one of race and ethnicity, as the lower-resourced areas in many U.S. cities and regions have a higher concentration of racially diverse populations that historically have been marginalized and oppressed. Universal access does not necessarily translate to "equal access." From a legal standpoint, however, Universal Preschool has the potential to address access issues, but only with sustained financial commitment. Gomez-Velez (2015) points out, "Whether universal pre-kindergarten can overcome extreme race and income segregation to reach low-income children of color depends on legal infrastructure and sufficient, equitable, and sustained fiscal commitment" (p. 354).

Ladson-Billings (2004) highlights the influence of race on policy as follows: "Issues of race and racism permeate U.S. culture—through law, language, politics, economics, symbols, art, public policy—and the prevalence of race is not merely in those spaces [which are] seen as racially defined spaces" (p. 5). This discourse of universal access, while not explicitly "about" race, is, as Ladson-Billings suggests, "permeated" with race. As larger social movements, discursive formations, and individual stories are considered, perhaps the presence of racial, as well as other social inequities, will become more visible and concrete. The social inequity of affordable housing and homelessness affects many young children and their families. Yet, national, state, and local policies create potholes for families who seek to access programs and services. While public schools and Head Start are required to provide services for those they serve who are experiencing homelessness, other parts of the early childhood system receive little funding or support to assist families with this need.

In the search to better understand the power dynamics and politics at play, with an eye to the individual, and the impact of culture, race, economics, and experiences of each person, the policy process can be seen as just that: a process that continues to question who is served by the policy and to what end. Perhaps, too, these suggestions not only apply to the Universal Preschool process but also shed light on current K–12 public policy in the United States. These enrollment stories illustrate on various levels (federal, local, and individual) the complexity of Universal Preschool policy and the importance of understanding self within the larger social context, thus illuminating the paradox of public education.

REFLECTIVE CONVERSATIONS AND ACTIONS

1. Choices for families with young children are important, considering that many parents and other family caregivers work and need full-day services. Why is it important to develop Universal Preschool programs that include Head Start, school districts, early education and care programs, and related community providers?

2. Targeted preschool offerings and compensatory programs have shown across time that children gain academically and have provided an opportunity to avoid the achievement gap or, as Gloria Ladson-Billings suggests, begin to pay "the education debt" (Ladson-Billings, 2006; see also Fuller, 2014). How is it possible to provide universal access and honor targeted programs? Is it important to maintain programs as they have existed through segregated funding streams or is it more important to honor the notion of being inclusive across all demographics, offering program choice and access to all children? Is it possible to do both? How?

3. Families with young children with disabilities often have hard choices in deciding where their children will attend preschool. Often special education services are offered only at school district sites that may not be convenient. What options might there be in a Universal Preschool collaborative for more choices for families of preschoolers with disabilities?

4. It is very common for family members to work outside the home with limited availability for large parts of the day. Yet, many public preschool programs operate only 4 days a week and for limited hours. In addition, there are a variety of cultures, languages, and living arrangements represented among families. How can Universal Preschool programs engage in a variety of communication strategies with families to ensure access and participation?

5. Using the resources below as a starting place, craft insights on how the debate regarding compensatory education fits into the move toward universal access. How might programs using specific enrollment criteria fit into a universal plan? How can we ensure we are providing supports needed for all children in equitable ways?

   • Fuller, B. (2014, February 9). Preschool is important, but it's more important for poor children. Retrieved from www.washingtonpost.com/opinions/preschool-is-important-but-its-more-important-for-poor-children/2014/02/09/79ff4ab4-8e96-11e3-b227-12a45d109e03_story.html?utm_term=.bc487d909b71

   • Beatty, B. (2012). Rethinking compensatory education: Historical perspectives on race, class, culture, language, and the discourse of the "disadvantaged child." *Teachers College Record 14*(6), 1–11. Retrieved from www.tcrecord.org/content.asp?contentid=16688

   • Barnett, W. S., Brown, K., & Shore, R. (2004). *The universal vs. targeted debate: Should the United States have preschool for all?* (Policy Brief, Issue 6). New Brunswick, NJ: National Institute for Early Education Research. Retrieved from nieer.org/wp-content/uploads/2016/08/6.pdf

CHAPTER 5

Leading the Curriculum Process

"Education is not preparation for life; education is life itself."

—John Dewey

Collaborative leadership is often viewed as a cornerstone for democratic policy processes; however, as we show in this chapter, this form of shared communication also can create confusion. Clarity regarding curriculum and its implementation for teaching offers one example of leadership ambiguity and possibility. The process of learning to lead in a collaborative environment is an education in itself, specifically in terms of how teachers engage with curriculum.

We use curriculum choice, planning, and the implementation process to illustrate the divergent, and at times confusing, nature of collaborative leadership (Strauss, 2002). Insights gleaned include teachers' increased confidence in autonomous curriculum interpretation and the influence of individual agency policy and context on multi-agency collaborations.

CURRICULUM IN EARLY EDUCATION

In early childhood education, curriculum most often takes the form of child-initiated projects facilitated by the teacher (Helm & Katz, 2016; Petersen, 2003; Seefeldt & Wasik, 2006). It is common practice to center on the child and, using developmental theory and knowledge of family and community contexts, build learning experiences that allow for inquiry and exploration toward new knowledge (Berk & Winsler, 1995; Copple & Bredekamp, 2009; Delaney, Whyte, & Graue, 2020; Heimer & Winokur, 2015). At the same time, the use of standards as a means to measure student success is gaining traction in the early years. This results in administrators, teachers, and families feeling increased pressure to ensure that children are meeting academic benchmarks before entering formal school settings. Adding this academic push-down philosophy, while honoring previously acknowledged best practices in early education, is challenging for many early educators (Brown, Mowry, & Feger, 2015; Christakis, 2016; Fuller, 2007). This pressure to align early childhood curriculum with standards to ensure that preschoolers are academically "ready for school" mirrors K–12 educational system approaches (Michael-Luna et al., 2019; National Governors Association Center for Best Practices & Council of Chief State School Officers, 2010). Applying upper-grade-level curricular content and pedagogy does not take into consideration the unique developmental and cultural needs of each young child, nor does it honor how young children learn (Goldstein, 2007; Heimer & Klefstad, 2015). This is further complicated by statewide systems that separate development levels (K–12 and early childhood) by department (education and health and human services). This creates myriad standards, guidelines, and requirements that may have conflicting guidance, especially for Universal Preschool programs. Recent research suggests the need to consider implementation beyond standards and child outcomes to include consideration of administrative and instructional practices (Graue, Ryan, Wilinski, Northey, & Nocera, 2018).

There are increasing efforts to create early learning standards through national organizations (such as NAEYC) and on a state-by-state basis (e.g., New York, Wisconsin, Massachusetts, among others) to use in lesson planning and assessment, similar to the Common Core State Standards (CCSS) for later grades (Brown, 2007; Mueller & File, 2020). Many Universal Preschool programs are modifying their curricula due to this pressure toward an academic push-down of standardization, accountability, and skill demonstration (Au & Ferrare, 2015; Spencer, 2014).

A key discourse between collaborative partners often involves how and what young children should learn. Those partners with a strong background in child development, with concentration in the early years, suggest that young children learn best through hands-on experiences that inspire creativity, experimentation, and problem solving in an atmosphere of trusting and supportive relationships. Other partners may believe that the greatest need is to prepare young children for "school readiness." To an early childhood professional, the concept of school readiness can result in a diminishing sense of the importance of best practices for young children. In the end, children are the ones who lose the potential of deeply satisfying and enjoyable early learning experiences.

There is danger in this push-down of curriculum, assessment methods, and teaching practices. The pedagogy for young children is different than for older children; therefore, the approaches to knowledge acquisition must be unique (Bodrova & Leong, 2007; Copple & Bredekamp, 2009; Helm & Katz, 2016; Wisnewski & Reifel, 2012). Many early childhood curriculum products are child-centered and culturally relevant; however, implementation with fidelity in preschool programs is questionable due to accountability pressures. A similar situation occurs with assessment of children. Assessing the "whole child" can be lost in the alignment of standards across developmental domains. This approach also may miss the mark on ensuring practices that are age-appropriate, sensitive to cultural differences, and unique to individual children. Some critics also suggest that in centering developmentally appropriate practices, Western notions of development are privileged in a way that creates an additive versus authentic approach to supporting cultural and linguistic diversity (Bloch, Swadener, & Cannella, 2014; Brown & Lan, 2015; Grieshaber

& Cannella, 2001; Nelson, 2009; Smith, 2015). Early childhood educators become the link for interpreting and connecting across cultural experiences.

Pinar's (2004) notion of centering self in society is helpful when considering the role of the teacher in early childhood. He suggests, "Teaching—from the point of view of curriculum theory—is a matter of enabling students to employ academic knowledge . . . to understand their own self-formation within society and the world" (p. 16). The idea of integrating the learning of academic content with an awareness of self and others corresponds with the desires of teachers of young children. Gloria Ladson-Billings (2004) defines culturally relevant pedagogy using a three-pronged approach that requires (1) academic learning, (2) development of cultural competence, and (3) sociopolitical or critical consciousness. Many teachers seek to find the balance between academic achievement and the need to foster socioemotional and cultural understandings.

Both Pinar's philosophy of curriculum and the description we have shared regarding the current debates in early childhood education run counter to the current movement toward standardization of learning through testing and narrowing the curriculum with a focus on academic outcomes. Academic gains and honoring early education pedagogy are not mutually exclusive. This brings us back to the idea of leadership. How do teachers navigate the choice

Engaged in Learning

and implementation of curriculum in this complex context, with the added ambiguity of multi-site, multi-agency influence?

CHILD PERSPECTIVE

My uncle gave me a giant yellow ball for my fifth birthday, and we had fun playing together at my party! I like playing with all kinds of balls—big ones, small ones, heavy ones, and bouncy ones. My friend Marta likes to play catch with me outside and we have lots of fun. I learned that balls are round and they come in many colors. I also figured out that some balls bounce higher than others. I like playing with real balls. Coloring a ball red on a piece of paper is not as much fun, but my teacher says I have to do it so she knows I'm ready for kindergarten.

PAST STORY: ECC—WHO'S THE BOSS?

One of the dilemmas I faced teaching in a new 4-year-old kindergarten public school collaboration with Head Start was figuring out who was my supervisor. There were many people involved in the collaboration, yet no clear leader.

- A researcher told me about the position and helped me get started by discussing classroom set-up and schedule. I thought she was my boss.
- The school district lead principal hired me for the 4-year-old kindergarten pilot and guided me through the procedural steps in the system. I thought she was my boss.
- The research graduate student, an experienced early childhood educator who took fieldnotes and observed in the classroom, talked to me frequently regarding daily issues. I thought she was my boss.
- The district early childhood specialist talked with me about the curriculum she helped choose for the pilot. I thought she was my boss.
- The school principal, the person in the school to whom I reported, felt that the university researcher was leading the pilot and that I was in good hands. So, was he my boss?
- Then I learned about the Abbot Center director, who was assigned as head teacher for the pilot to give support to our classrooms. Aha, I thought, I'd found my boss. And yet she often cancelled and then stopped coming.

Each of these "supervisors" had knowledge and information I found useful; however, because there were so many people involved and there were no designated leaders, it was difficult to understand whom I should seek out for guidance. In the end, I realized I was my own boss (Rebekah Carpenter, Greentree teacher).

Collaboratives or community partnerships have been suggested as a strategy to meet the needs of young children, and in doing so, avoid an achievement gap in later years. However, as this vignette illustrates, the leadership of this past Universal Preschool endeavor was confusing. This ultimately resulted in the teachers becoming their own leaders.

Leadership and Communication in the Pilot Program

As the UPK pilot collaboration progressed, issues of leadership, decisionmaking, and focus of control arose, specifically around choice and implementation of curriculum. The pilot consisted of two sites, one at Greentree Elementary and one at Waterfront Head Start, with oversight by the respective agencies, as well as broad direction by a university researcher at the Abbott Center (one research arm of the local university) (see Figure 5.1). With two sites sharing curricula but located within separate agencies, leadership and information dissemination emerged as a concern.

Communication in the pilot collaborative changed between fall and spring. At the beginning of the school year, people were discussing what it meant to be part of a "collaboration" and establishing the goals of the pilot. During the first year, each teacher asked questions of the researchers regarding their roles in the collaboration, more specifically addressing issues of frequency of communication with pilot staff. Given these questions, Rebekah, the Greentree teacher (in her first year of teaching), found it helpful to create a chart detailing the lines of communication over the course of the school year. According to her chart, initially there were 26 lines of consistent communication (at least biweekly) among staff, which included cooks, bus drivers, teacher aides, teachers, principals, directors, researchers, and so on. Infrequent communication (less than once a month) also was occurring among the same number of people. As the year went on, the lines of consistent communication dropped dramatically from 26 to three. The lines that remained were between the classroom teachers. While communication was streamlined, the reporting lines between personnel remained complicated, and there was no explicit communication to the teachers regarding the change in frequency of meetings. Rebekah, Pam, and the Greentree social worker met regularly to "collaborate," but became less sure of what this meant as the year went on. By the end of the year, teachers and social workers felt they should just focus on their own classrooms and families, and stop trying to make the cross-site "collaboration" happen.

Policy Interpretations. As we return to the notions of policy as text and discourse, the perspective of this UPK partnership illuminates certain freedoms as well as limitations regarding the impact of leadership on teachers' understandings of curriculum. As a reminder, we are defining policy as both a text (literal

Figure 5.1. UPK Pilot Leadership Structure

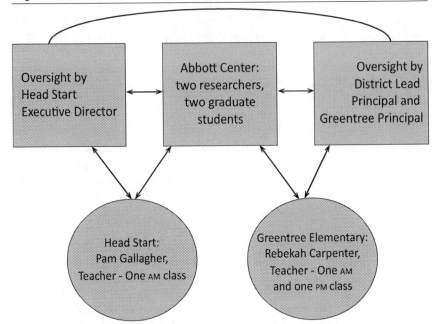

yet interpretive text) and discourse (the influence of structural power on the individual to articulate and constrain policy meaning) (Ball, 1994).

This definition suggests that individuals not only follow the text of policy but also interpret policy in particular ways in their practice, based in part on larger discourses at play. The tension that is created resides in the teacher's interpretation of policy as seen in individual action/reaction; however, it is important to recognize the larger discourses that may constrain teachers in their freedom to enact policy. The curriculum policy illustrates how the dynamic of individual freedom within agency discourses complicated the notion of uniform leadership for a collaborative project (Michael-Luna, Heimer, & Grey, 2020). How did the leadership function in this collaboration?

Leadership Communication Matters. In February of the first year of the pilot, a meeting was held to bring together the key players (principal, district's lead elementary principal, researchers [absent], teachers, social workers, Head Start executive, and associate directors) in the collaboration to reflect on the progress of the pilot. Participants were asked to reflect on:

- Collaboration at the agency and family levels
- Recruitment for enrollment
- Curriculum
- Assessment

In this meeting, many concerns were raised regarding the communication and effectiveness of the collaboration. The key concerns were more clearly defining the mission and philosophy of the pilot, as well as clarifying the roles of each staff member. It also was suggested that a leader or co-facilitator for group meetings would be helpful. Although the results of this meeting were shared with all and forwarded to those absent, it was unclear what action would be taken or who would address the concerns. Multiple leaders with agency involvement created an image of collaboration; however, there was no motivation or movement to clarify "who was the boss." This leadership structure functioned within an *enacted partnership* model (Seddon, Billett, & Clemans, 2005). Therefore, though the outcomes were beneficial to all stakeholders the communication was vertical (there were multiple named leaders). However, the horizontal policy made for ambiguous communication and lack of direction for the teachers.

Curriculum in the Pilot

The leaders of the pilot chose the Creative Curriculum and Doors to Discovery as the primary curricula (Dodge, Colker, & Heroman, 2002). These two programs offered different approaches to curriculum and each was meant to complement the other. The Creative Curriculum, while comprehensive in many ways (outlining environments, schedules, projects, and unit ideas), was a more open-ended resource for the teachers and was presented in one book. Doors to Discovery was presented as a boxed set that offered units in a suggested order throughout the year and included materials for reproduction, books linked to the units, activity suggestions tied to skills learned, and CDs with related songs, among other support material. The Creative Curriculum provided a foundation or guiding philosophy. However, the Doors to Discovery material was integrated in a more prescriptive and visible fashion. The leadership team (which varied depending on the meeting) wanted the teachers to uniquely implement the curriculum allowing freedom for teacher interpretation.

The leaders of the pilot were regular participants at planning meetings. They offered concrete instructions for teachers (specific curriculum packages) and charts outlining tasks, persons responsible, and completion dates for pilot committee members. Many of the monthly curriculum projects and units, while not implemented simultaneously, were covered in both sites (e.g., community, backyard adventure, cooking), although some months teachers created their own topics (fall, water wonderland).

Based on interviews, observations, and input from the teachers, there was an appreciation for having materials provided (Doors to Discovery) that they could adapt to meet the needs of their students. However, there was some confusion regarding administrators' expectations for adapting the curriculum. Therefore, each teacher had her own explanation for the curriculum choices she made in the classroom.

Two themes emerged around curriculum: (1) the unique way each teacher evolved as an autonomous leader of curriculum, and (2) the impact of agency policy on curriculum implementation. As teachers refined their understanding of curriculum, the questions of collaborative leadership and who was in charge surfaced once again:

- Who chose the curriculum?
- Who was responsible for training or orienting the teachers to the new curriculum?
- Who decided the mission of the pilot?
- Who was leading this collaborative process?

Often, the discussion regarding curriculum began with questioning what is being assessed, how it is measured, and what the assessment means for the child. The quote below outlines the difficult nature of assessing young children's knowledge, skills, and abilities. The teacher had been given an assessment to use, and while she shared the merits for the child and the program, there were uncertainties about the accuracy and the purpose of focused recall.

A parent came in with her [daughter's] report card and she said, "It says [something like] draw a figure with 8 to 10 body parts, well my daughter only had 7. What should I do to teach her to draw the other body parts?" And I said, "No, no. Please don't drill her on drawing the body," and I think that was my concern about the progress report, although it also brought some parents in to discuss these issues. . . . I felt like the challenge was to figure out how to do [the assessment]. Maybe it was a little too academic focused [knowledge of body parts]. I felt like then I ended up kind of doing a test. (Rebekah Carpenter, Greentree teacher)

Rebekah defaulted to teaching through skill assessment as she was unclear where the specific knowledge or skills were taught in the curriculum. Assessment is directly linked to curriculum. What we teach, how we teach it, and how this is communicated to children, families, and administrators, are the areas of focus in terms of policy interpretation and leadership influence.

Impact of Collaborative Leadership on Curriculum Implementation

In the assessment vignette, Rebekah expressed frustration over reconciling her teaching beliefs and strategies with communicating the outcomes to families.

Her frustration continued as she implemented the curriculum and sought approval from leaders of the collaborative.

> It was the second time I had used the Doors to Discovery sounds and letters materials. . . . Each child was looking for the letter M in a poem. They had a Post-it® with the letter M on it and when they found one in the poem, they placed the Post-it® on top. Susan, the district early childhood specialist, walked in as the last few students were putting up their letters. She beamed her contagious smile and looked content with the class. I was proud of myself that I had used the sounds and letters book and that Susan actually saw me teaching from it.
>
> A few days later, Susan came back for a check-in meeting about what she had observed. . . . She explained how happy she was to see so much of the children's work up on the walls at a level where they could see and touch it. . . . I was really on the right track here. However, she then explained that it was really unnecessary to work on letter recognition . . . as it will emerge naturally in a literacy-rich environment. . . . I didn't really understand. Hadn't the pilot planning group decided on that curriculum? . . . Didn't they give it to me so I would use it? Hadn't they talked [to one another]? I felt so betrayed because I had thought there was a group of people who had made decisions about how they envisioned this curriculum being used. . . . I was realizing that no one was really working together to figure this out. I never took out the sounds and letters book again. (Rebekah Carpenter, Greentree teacher)

At the beginning of the year, Rebekah received the Creative Curriculum and eight boxes of Doors to Discovery materials, each one with a different themed literacy unit, and was told these were the curricula chosen by the pilot program leadership to be implemented in the classroom. She implemented what she thought was the expected curriculum. However, as the vignette on sounds and letters illustrates, this was a trial-and-error process, and she felt she was getting mixed messages. Susan had influence as she had taught preschool in this district in the past, and Rebekah respected her opinion. When asked about the resources and constraints of a packaged curriculum (Doors to Discovery), Rebekah shared:

> It's got really good ideas and . . . it's got interesting ways of setting up the day and it gives you explanations and it's easy to follow. The constraint would be that it's hard for me to then sit down and brainstorm and use my own creative mind because there's something there that I can depend on. . . . By May, I was more comfortable in my teaching. Once I was a little more settled I was able to say, "Well, actually I don't like this activity. I'm going to look somewhere else and see what other butterfly activities there are." (Rebekah Carpenter, Greentree teacher, October 2003)

Just before students began class in September, Rebekah met with the university researcher who also helped choose the curriculum and assisted Rebekah in setting up the daily schedule and organizing small groups and curriculum. She met with other researchers about ordering supplies, organizing donated supplies, and developing the different centers. About a month after school started, the district's early childhood specialist, Susan, came to talk to Pam and Rebekah about the curriculum, but there was no formal training. When Rebekah asked the research assistant, principal, and university faculty about Creative Curriculum, she was told she was on the right track and to use it as the backdrop for her classroom, but she was offered little additional information. In November, the teachers at both sites, researcher, and school social worker visited another school that was implementing Doors to Discovery. It was at this point that Rebekah began to recognize her power in the curriculum process. She shared:

> Ann Ford and Susan took a step back from the project after the first semester. Although they were available for phone calls and emails, direct influence on the curriculum decreased significantly. For me, as a new teacher to preschool with a desire to better understand what collaboration meant, this hands-off approach to leadership created a gap between the classroom and the curriculum policy. (Rebekah Carpenter, Greentree teacher, 2004)

Rebekah was looking for guidance regarding the academic nature of her lessons. As a teacher in her first year, she was looking for reassurance to know she was on the right track.

> I think the curriculum is pretty good. You know how far to go with it to provide balance between academics versus traditional developmentally appropriate play. I know they're learning through play but they're also learning through the academic literacy work from Doors to Discovery. I don't know how much to push it. (Rebekah Carpenter, Greentree teacher, October 2003)

Rebekah was looking for someone (the pilot leadership) to tell her what this balance would look like in her classroom. More than superficial affirmations, Rebekah wanted clear direction. As a previous quote illustrated, her perception of the lack of clear direction from a leader caused her to change her practice ("I never took out the sounds and letters book again."). She also felt an added pressure to have the children achieve academic success, as they were part of a research study. Pilot researchers measured the social development of children using the Child Assessment Profile (CAP) and the Social Skills Rating Scale (SSRS); they also used the Woodcock-Johnson Tests of Cognitive Abilities—an early childhood assessment of literacy skills—to pre- and posttest students. In the executive summary to the school board at the end of the pilot year, academic achievements were highlighted, indicating that literacy skills improved substantially for the majority of students. Even so, Rebekah still questioned whether her approach to the curriculum was what the pilot leadership had wanted.

In each of the interviews with Pam, the Head Start teacher (in her third year of teaching), her concern regarding the welfare of her students came through. She recounted the details of each child, and her eyes danced with joy as she talked about her relationships with the children. When the subject turned to curriculum, she paused and hesitated. When asked about her teaching philosophy, she responded:

> ...just doing my best to try to make the learning fun, picking up on what the kids are interested in and making it something that they enjoy instead of just, you know, sitting down, this is what we're going to do. (Pam Gallagher, Waterfront Head Start teacher, October 2003)

Pam suggested that her approach to teaching was more "open-ended than structured." In the following quote, her perception was that there was a "right" and a "wrong" way when discussing curriculum. She was a confident and capable teacher, yet apologized for not implementing the curriculum fully. Perhaps the Creative Curriculum approach would have resonated for Pam; however, Rebekah had begun the Doors to Discovery units and because this was one collaborative initiative with two sites, they were trying to be consistent. While it was understood that there would be unique aspects to each program, expectations existed for some uniformity.

> Well, we have the Doors to Discovery and right now I've been really bad at not [*sic*] following it [laughs]. . . . It's not that I don't like the curriculum, it's just hard to get into using something new when you have so many ideas of your own. . . . There was a week where we were doing the "new faces, new places," and we were outside and the kids were talking about the ladybugs, so then the next week we just totally switched it and went to a ladybug week. So I guess that's the biggest thing, is just going on the kids' interests. (Pam Gallagher, Waterfront Head Start teacher, October 2003)

In this excerpt, Pam shared about the difficult nature of implementing a curriculum package such as Doors to Discovery and still allowing the interests of the children to influence her planning. Emergent curriculum, and following the interests of children, is common pedagogical practice in early childhood and is something she did in the past. In July, after the end of the school year, she provided great detail about key components of the curriculum that she implemented. In her final interview, she shared:

> ...but it ended up that I really did like it [Doors to Discovery]. . . . It got the kids . . . reading and enjoying stories. I mean, it was cool to see them

Kids' Interests

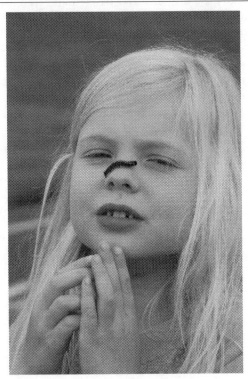

pick up the Tabby Tiger book and read it, because they memorized it, knew the stories, so that was pretty cool and I don't think that's something I would have thought of doing, like reading one story for a whole week ... without having it being introduced to me from Doors to Discovery. (Pam Gallagher, Waterfront Head Start teacher, July 2004)

Pam naturally tailored the lessons to the needs of her students, using the central character, Tabby. She articulated the successful aspects of the Doors to Discovery curriculum in terms of the children and their interests. Although we discussed the curriculum package and lesson plans, it was obvious that Pam also emphasized social and emotional support for the children. She felt that her primary role was to ensure that children felt welcome. She expanded on the need for children to learn empathy and then ended her thoughts about curriculum by discussing children learning the ABCs and their names, "things they would need to know for kindergarten." Across the span of the interviews from October to the following July, Pam explicitly connected her philosophy with the chosen curriculum. However, she suggested that her collaboration with her Head Start co-teacher and her strength as a teacher connecting with the children held the most importance for her teaching. This suggests her ability to teach the curriculum in terms of her strong relationship with children (Gittell, 2008). When describing herself as a teacher, she emphasized her accessibility and openness with the children:

> I always greet them with a hello and a smile and ask how they are. If the child feels comfortable, I always greet them with a hug or have them give me a high five because I'd always stand outside the door when the bus came in and greeted each and every one of them. I just made sure that they knew that they could come to me any time they wanted and ask me any questions. (Pam Gallagher, Waterfront Head Start teacher, 2004)

Pam continued to focus on the child at the center of her interactions. While she was implementing some of the pilot preschool curriculum, she did not recognize the connections between academics and social–emotional interactions as a curricular choice.

Self-Leadership as a Survival Strategy. Although initially the notion of "freedom" to implement the curriculum seemed daunting, eventually each teacher used the curriculum in ways she felt were best for the children. Paradoxically, Rebekah felt limited by the freedom to interpret the curriculum, while Pam felt limited by the constraints of a packaged curriculum. However, as the year progressed, both teachers were more confident interpreting Doors to Discovery without training or guidance, as evidenced in the quotes. The teachers' perceptions of their power to interpret the curriculum changed drastically over the course of the year. As each teacher interpreted the curriculum policy, it became obvious that her own personality and areas of interest influenced how the units were interpreted and presented to the children. We teach who we are (Palmer, 1994). The teachers were able to express their individual power through the choices they made regarding curriculum. This illustrates shared decisionmaking (teachers made curriculum choices) and working toward shared goals (coordinating the use of the Doors to Discovery curriculum at two sites). "Partnerships are judged more on the extent to which they support individuals and enhance their capacity to learn from their experience in ways that return tangible benefits" (Seddon, Billett, & Clemans, 2005, p. 571). In this example, the benefit was the growth that happened as a result of the collaborative yet autonomous work of the teachers.

Although there was a leadership deficit in bringing the two programs together, one of the most beneficial aspects of this freedom was each teacher's recognition of her autonomy. Within this broad understanding of freedom to implement the curriculum, each teacher gained more confidence in what she viewed as appropriate curriculum, and expressed her power through these choices.

Fluid Nature of Power. Although both teachers made discoveries about themselves, the way they reacted to the freedom took two separate forms. When faced with dilemmas requiring support, Pam turned to Head Start, while Rebekah referenced the leaders of the pilot. While the collaboration shifted some of Pam's practices, it was seen primarily as an extra component to her work. For example, in her interviews, she mentioned an interest in High Scope training. In addition, she talked about trying to better connect High Scope and Doors to Discovery. High Scope often is used in Head Start settings and includes a "plan–do–review" process. Teachers guide children in this process to encourage their purposeful engagement with activities and materials in specific interest centers. Pam said she would "overcome" the curriculum policy but quickly corrected herself to say "follow" the policy. She was more autonomous in relation to the pilot curriculum because she also had support from Head Start to use the existing High Scope curriculum.

In May, Rebekah suggested that having clearer goals for the pilot would have been helpful in terms of leadership. She felt that if pilot leaders had shared more about how the two sites worked together, the rationale for enrollment, and an overview of the broader context, her teaching would have been positively impacted. Gittell and Douglass (2012) take these ideas one step further to suggest that "relational leadership requires workers and managers to develop shared goals, shared knowledge and mutual respect fostering attentiveness to the emerging situation and to one another" (p. 720). Although both teachers expressed an interest in understanding "goals," they were looking to two different sources for answers.

This is one example of the fluid nature of power. While the leaders chose the curriculum, and the curriculum packages contained implementation directions, it was the teachers who independently determined what was most appropriate for their students.

Leadership Within and Across Agencies. With the dual implementation of Doors to Discovery and Creative Curriculum, teachers at each site had their own set of agency policies and personalities to consider. Head Start had curriculum protocol already in place using High Scope in addition to other policies, such as a required weekly food experience for the children. In addition, the program was housed in a duplex within the neighborhood of the families it served. The staff at Waterfront Head Start included a cook who interacted with the children throughout the day. This "home" environment, with scents of breakfast and lunch wafting throughout the house, created a unique setting.

Greentree, on the other hand, was housed within the K–5 school building. The classroom was downstairs near the cafeteria so it is feasible that the "scents" might have been just as home-like as at Head Start; however, it was clear that the kids were most excited about going to a "real" school on the "big kids" bus. In this setting, there were interactions with older kids, rules like silence in the halls, and a playground shared with "big kids."

I believe five different members of the pilot collaboration handed me the early learning standards. It was almost comical how every time I introduced myself as the new teacher in the pilot at Greentree to someone who I saw as a leader of the collaborative, he or she would hand me this thin yellow book with the standards. The standards provide a "framework for understanding and communicating a common set of expectations for young children's development within this context of shared responsibility" [Early Childhood Collaborative & Arborville School District, 2003, p. 1]. I was made to believe these were very important to the group; however as with most of the curricula I saw, it was handed to me by many [people], but not discussed with me. (Rebekah Carpenter, Greentree teacher)

As mentioned earlier, although Rebekah worried about academics in her curriculum, she quickly learned from the kindergarten teachers at Greentree that there was a strong focus on having students feel comfortable with the school routine.

Teachers in kindergarten are telling me no, what they need is kids who listen to directions ... especially the ones who don't have siblings or have never been in a program before ... sharing and working in teams and those kind of things. (Rebekah Carpenter, Greentree teacher, May 2004)

She continued to share her belief that she had met those goals:

I think that the majority of kids are used to the routine, they're used to the school, they are ready to be working in draft books because of the journaling. They're a lot better about raising their hands, they have skills that they will need in kindergarten. They're used to small groups and doing more of a directed activity, so I think that they have a lot of the skills that they'll need for kindergarten. (Rebekah Carpenter, Greentree teacher, May 2004)

Working in the school where the children would attend kindergarten, she recognized the kindergarten teachers as leaders in terms of offering her direction in the K–5 school setting. She continued to work with these teachers in the same school and shared a sense of responsibility to prove how important UPK would be to the students' future learning. Similar to Pam, Rebekah came to see her setting as offering the most support beyond the multi-agency collaborative.

Both in March and in July, Pam suggested that children having fun learning was her most important consideration. Particularly for Pam, children needed to feel safe and happy:

Always hearing that they want to come back tomorrow is a highlight and it makes your day. Just seeing them smile and seeing them having a good time is what's important to me. I think it is important to give them that environment where they know Kaia [assistant teacher] and I want to see them every day and want them to come back. (Pam Gallagher, Waterfront Head Start teacher, March 2004)

It is not clear whether this relationship with the children comes directly from her experience working with Head Start, but Head Start places a significant policy emphasis on the importance of the social and emotional experience for the children.

In relation to the impact of Head Start policy on her classroom, Pam mentioned the fact that in order to meet the pilot requirements, her class shifted from a 3- to 5-year-old, mixed-age group to 4- and 5-year-olds only. While she welcomed this change, she also mentioned more than once the pressure placed on her and the social worker to enroll at least 18 children. The school year started with a class of 14 children. The class size of 18 is determined by federal policy; however, individual agencies interpret and follow this to varying degrees. There is a threat from the federal level to close programs that do not fully enroll on a consistent basis.

Finally, considering the assessments required for Head Start and additional assessments for the pilot, it became clear that the pilot was a supplement to an existing program. In other words, Pam was already required to provide multiple assessments of children using the Child Observation Record, as suggested by Head Start's High Scope curriculum. Therefore, the requirement to do the CAP and the SSRS, as well as assist with family interviews, created additional work in relation to her teaching and assessment.

Curriculum, Collaboration, and Agency Policy

Both Head Start and Greentree are governed by large bureaucracies and yet there were specific contextual differences for the two sites. This leads to consideration of broad agency policy influence and the immediate contextual influence on the implementation of curriculum.

The ability of teachers to interpret broad policy directives was found at each of the sites. According to Rebekah, the early learning standards booklet became the district curriculum policy for her, while Pam looked to others at Head Start for policy direction. At a literal level, this represents curriculum policy as text (Ball, 1994). However, these agency policy texts were never read by the teachers; rather, they were understood via the leadership. The influential discourse for Rebekah was developmentally appropriate practice and the early learning standards, while Pam's was High Scope. In other words, the policies themselves are rarely consulted, but it is through interpretation and the influence of surrounding discourses that policy is implemented (Ball, 1994). This corresponds to the idea of multiple discourses circulating and coming together to form a grid of reasoning (Popkewitz, 1998). Consideration of a "grid" of discourses allows movement beyond the influence of one discourse to consider multiple influences on classroom practice and, in this example, curriculum implementation within public school and Head Start sites.

Although the pilot allowed freedom to interpret the curriculum within policy and agency constraints, it also limited some freedoms of implementation. These outward (context) as well as elusive (standards and policy) influences impacted how the curriculum was implemented for the pilot. Therefore, the teachers were left to interpret the agency influence without clear direction from the leadership of the pilot. Did it matter if some of the classroom rules were different? Did it matter if the focus was on academics? The curriculum policy, although offering a range of possibilities, was still bound by each teacher's understanding of the expectations of her employer.

The collaborative leadership approach allowed for autonomy and yet the teachers felt there were expectations, expressed as "academic pressure" by Rebekah, or a prescribed philosophy (High Scope) by Pam. This pressure is embedded in the larger discourses of the public school and Head Start. Pam was more comfortable relying on her experience and professional knowledge as a connective thread, while Rebekah, as a teacher new to preschool, was less confident relying on her own abilities.

Both individual and agency influence on the curriculum was either taken up or rejected. The power of each teacher's interpretation of curriculum created unique classrooms. However, they both desired to better understand the meaning of "collaboration." In other words, although the level of concern varied between the teachers, there was a desire to feel more a part of the "collaborative" process, beyond having the freedom to interpret curriculum.

PRESENT STORY: WHO GETS TO SAY WE CAN PLAY IN 4K?

Katherine K. Delaney

In this case study, one teacher, Wanda, struggles to implement her school district's vision of a child-centered, play-based 4K within the context of her school. Wanda works in a Title 1 school, Fuji Elementary, listed by the state as "a school in need of improvement" due to low proficiency scores in math and reading. The school serves a predominantly low-income population in a mid-sized university town. Many of the students are English language learners, including refugees and recent immigrants.

Within this context, Wanda's school leader is focused on how she can utilize the new 4K year as a tool to improve student readiness for 5K and beyond. Wanda, who was a kindergarten teacher at Fuji for 10 years prior to moving to 4K, understands the pressure for readiness at the start of kindergarten. However, she also has chosen to move into 4K because she feels that the readiness and academic focus of kindergarten that has evolved during her teaching is developmentally inappropriate. Wanda's hope is that in 4K she will be able to practice in ways that reflect her early childhood pedagogical beliefs.

However, almost immediately, Wanda begins to see how the complexities of 4K within a school system create complicated realities for her practice. Since 4K is under the umbrella of "early childhood" within the district, Wanda has many expectations to manage outside of her own school setting, including parents whose children are in this first year of 4K. This story is a bit about "who's the boss," but also about competing visions and needs for the 4K year.

At a required summer workshop for incoming 4K teachers, a little less than a month prior to the start of the school year, a large conference ballroom is filled to the brim. District representatives from the Early Childhood Department are walking the teachers through how 4K should be different from kindergarten: limited whole-group instruction, no calendar time, lots of choices, learning through play, and active engagement. From their descriptions, 4K will look nothing like the kindergartens that exist a few doors down in the school buildings. Rather, these 4K classrooms will reflect a play-based, child-centered pedagogy, with the goal of responsive practices, rather than outcome-oriented interventions. While some of the teachers seem overjoyed at these statements, other teachers seem less excited. What the Early Childhood Department folks are asking for is that teachers fundamentally shift their approaches to teaching and engagement.

Wanda describes this meeting as a "total jaw dropper" and feels both nervous and excited about the opportunity before her. However, as the school year creeps along, Wanda's school leader, as well as the kindergarten teachers in her building who used to feel like her colleagues, now make comments about how much work they have to do to "get kids ready." Wanda's school leader, walking past her teeming, rowdy, and fully engaged classroom of 4-year-olds, furrows her brow and expresses concern that the children aren't learning in the ways that they need to in order to be successful in kindergarten. Similarly, Wanda spends time explaining to her families—some of whom she had in her previous kindergarten classroom—why 4K is seemingly so different from kindergarten. Many of her families, whose first educational experiences in the United States have been through their children, are confused as to why, if 4K is the start of school now, as 5K was before, the daily experiences of their children are so very different.

Much of Wanda's first year of 4K is spent working on her strong professional beliefs in play-based and child-centered practice for 4-year-olds. Yet, she also spends a good deal of energy attempting to balance these beliefs and practices against the more dominant narratives and expectations of district-level leaders and her peers at Fuji. In addition, Wanda is participating in a professional development project focused on integrating play-based and funds of knowledge–driven early mathematics into the 4K classroom. While the professional development seems to feed Wanda's own pedagogical beliefs, it also acts as another external expectation for practice.

Across the school year, Wanda balances these narratives, her own beliefs, and the clamorous voices of 30 4-year-olds (15 in the morning and 15 in the afternoon). While the outside voices seem louder, and more influential in the beginning, as Wanda settles into life with her 4-year-olds, their needs, wants, desires, and motivations come to be the lens through which she interprets her own pedagogical beliefs. This act—of placing children's voices at the forefront of decisionmaking—isn't seamless. Wanda struggles, sometimes pushing more teacher-centered and outcome-focused activities when her assessments are due, or when the children are about to be assessed for kindergarten readiness at the end of their 4K year. Overwhelmingly, though, as an experienced teacher, Wanda lets her own sense of what her students need direct her decisionmaking, protecting the 4K year from the goals of others.

SUMMARY

The "Past" and "Present" stories, although 15 years apart, are remarkably similar. The professional development offered through experts in early education or research centers differed from the advice of colleagues in school-based settings. As shared in Chapter 2, research suggests that appropriate, relevant, and responsive learning experiences will indeed begin to address gaps across student learning groups. Additionally, all teachers in the stories recognized the pressure for standardized approaches that more clearly aligned with traditional kindergarten programs. However, how the curriculum is chosen and implemented for these programs remains controversial, as it is interpreted by teachers influenced by diverse leadership structures.

I See You

Power Differentials and Clear Leadership

The collaborative leadership directives suggest sharing decisionmaking, responsibility, and costs equitably; however, in the "Past" and "Present" stories, there are power differentials between agencies that are not acknowledged. Power differentials exist and are reinforced through technologies of the self and the larger agency and societal discourses (Foucault, 1980). For example, the Abbott Center and district provided the funds for the pilot in the "Past" story. This resulted in deferring some decisionmaking to these agencies based on their financial power. Although agencies and individuals express certain levels of power, these levels may shift and change over time and in different contexts. For example, the teachers' ability to "improvise" (Graue, Whyte, & Delaney, 2014) and adapt the curriculum to fit the needs of the children, and honor their own pedagogical skills, suggests power in the autonomy offered to teachers in a collaborative process. The need to consider, through inquiry and analysis, the shifting nature of the power that individuals and agencies bring to each collaborative project is paramount for clear leadership.

Vision and Goals

Communication in all stages of planning is crucial, particularly for a collaborative process. The goals of the "Past" story collaborative, although written in terms of research or outcomes for children and families, did not rise to the surface in a concrete form for the teachers. The lack of understanding of how individual actions fit into the larger project works against a sense of "belonging" to the collaboration. Similarly, in the "Present" story, there were conflicting messages regarding curricular approaches. The curriculum approach emphasized during professional development was emergent in nature, while site-specific leaders stressed kindergarten readiness. With consideration of the three partnership models (enacted, community, and negotiated) it is understandable how shared goals were elusive as external agencies (district, university) had influence on the enactment of curriculum policy (Seddon, Billett, & Clemans, 2005). Ongoing evaluation and communication allow teachers to recognize how they fit into the project. Providing guiding principles for collaborative leadership, including fostering shared power and, more specifically, shared decisionmaking is imperative. Perhaps if there had been a briefing regarding independent or shared power, the teachers might have felt more at ease in their roles as independent decisionmakers and leaders.

Distributed Leadership

In terms of clarity, distributed leadership provides teachers some reference point to better understand their independence. Teachers historically have been immersed in a society of hierarchy (both explicit and implicit); therefore, the shift to perceived independence in our stories is questioned and accepted in varied ways. Gaining curricular confidence is one way teachers step into leadership as architects for change (Douglass, 2017).

We suggest distributed leadership as a transition from a more traditional hierarchical or authoritarian model to a collaborative model (Burch & Spillane, 2004; Good, 2018; Spillane, Halverson, & Diamond, 2001). Distributed leadership builds on the notion of communities of practice (Wenger, 1998) to offer an exchange of information and expertise across sites (Head Start, classrooms, district offices, etc.). Using this model, there are "middle managers" that perform a "brokering" role with multiple individuals and sites. These brokers perform tasks such as translating reform agendas for classroom staff; working with implementation and student outcome data to help teachers and principals improve instruction; designing staff development and training in terms of the reform; and creating routines and practices that connect specific expertise with other individuals (Burch & Spillane, 2004). In terms of both the "Past" and "Present" stories, this would have meant hiring a head teacher as well as assigning specific tasks to existing personnel to aid in communication and the transition to more classroom input in policy reform. Recognizing the value of "pooling expertise" to support group success over individual achievement provides new ways to lead across agencies (Burch & Spillane, 2004; Wenger 1998). This clarification of responsibility for specific individuals would provide support for enhanced communication at least in terms of the expectations for collaboration.

Concepts such as "inclusive" or "participatory" are problematic. However, radical change to traditional hierarchical decisionmaking requires the creation of different ways of understanding individual and group influences. Distributed and relational leadership offer this middle ground. Early childhood educators have more to gain from a policy reform process that takes into consideration the nuanced dynamics of power.

Collaboration Cautions

We caution writers of policy initiatives to carefully consider the notion that collaboration is a panacea for the democratic creation of early education programs. The greatest stumbling block, in our experience, is the ambiguous communication channels created by an amorphous definition of "collaboration." In addition, there are issues of individual and agency influences that warrant acknowledgment in terms of impact on implementing policy. These issues highlight examples of what Seddon, Billett, and Clemans (2004) refer to as role conflict, interest conflict, and regime conflict. If existing discourses of authority, as well as other power structures, are acknowledged as having influence throughout the policy process, then what is seen as "successful" curriculum or leadership can be considered in new ways (Selden et al., 2006). In addition, pulling from the strength of early educators to honor relationship building as a way to lead supports collaborative efforts (Gittell & Douglass, 2012). These new ways of considering the process allow for new possibilities for children.

REFLECTIVE CONVERSATIONS AND ACTIONS

1. What is your experience with the different approaches to curriculum between early education programs, Head Start, and K–12 settings? How did you relate to the experiences of Rebekah and Pam? In what ways do you work autonomously and in what ways do you rely on leaders in your organization to support the curriculum? How does this experience inform UPK policy?

2. Does your state have early learning standards? How are these used to create a uniform message on the developmental patterns of children and approaches to learning and curriculum? What are the pros and cons for the use of standards in the early years?

3. Have you ever had a situation where you were unclear about the vision and goals of an organization? Did you understand your role? What kinds of communication from leadership would have made it clearer?

4. Why is it important to have discussions with colleagues, families, and community members about curriculum that honors the whole child and values the benefits of play?

5. How might a leadership approach that honors the strength of relationships increase clarity while rolling out policy (e.g., curriculum policy)? How might a distributed leadership approach, as opposed to a hierarchical approach, support policy implementation for Universal Preschool? In what ways were both approaches present in the story with Pam and Rebekah? Why is the issue of leadership paramount in the Universal Preschool movement? What does collaboration have to do with it?

CHAPTER 6

A Long and Winding Road

"The most important thing to remember is this: To be ready at any moment to give up what you are for what you might become."

—W.E.B. DuBois

The path to Universal Preschool is not an easy one. Historical and societal detours have challenged this progress. Funding has been a constant roadblock, and although patches have been applied to the system, it is far from a smooth road. As changes are considered for next steps in Universal Preschool, we view power as part of the idea of letting go of current educational programming to consider what is possible in early childhood education and what the ECE system "might become." We suggest that the lessons learned in our Universal Preschool stories apply across educational systems, especially in terms of equity, leadership, and collaboration.

Equity is implied by the term *universal* and creates the umbrella under which our three stories of (1) collaboration, (2) access and enrollment, and (3) leadership and curriculum exist. From these stories, we gained greater understanding of policy in practice.

Three key insights for Universal Preschool guide this chapter:

1. Collaborative efforts are required in Universal Preschool, as this work is inherently cross-sector. It is important to honor and include all perspectives.
2. The term *UPK* (*Universal Prekindergarten*) is problematic, as it conflates early education (birth to age 5) with the K–12 system. Therefore, we suggest *Universal Preschool* as a more accurate term.
3. Universal Preschool offers an opportunity to address issues of equity in the United States, with recognition of power, assumptions, and discourses at play.

These insights frame the complexity of addressing strengths and barriers within the Universal Preschool movement, particularly in the areas of (1) collaborative leadership, (2) standardization and curriculum, and (3) exploration of the education debt as it relates to the achievement (or opportunity) gap.

Patience

NEXT STEPS ON THE UNIVERSAL PRESCHOOL JOURNEY

In previous chapters we outlined how "Past" and "Present" stories, although occurring 15 years apart, provide powerful lessons through their similarity. Families are still navigating a fragmented system to find services for their young children. Funding is still lacking and inconsistent. Questions continue to arise around appropriate curriculum for young children.

Where are we in our efforts to provide Universal Preschool in the United States? At the current rate of movement and change, it will take 75 years to reach kindergarten levels of enrollment for 4-year-olds in preschool and Head Start, and it will take 175 years for 3-year-olds (Friedman-Krauss et al., 2019). These time estimates do not account for program quality—it would likely take even longer to ensure that all children have access to high-quality preschool. If access to early education is the goal, these numbers indicate a need to consider more broadly how to structure our investments in early education.

The Centers for Disease Control and Prevention (CDC) identify early childhood education programs, such as preschool, as one of the most important

FAMILY PERSPECTIVE

We live on a farm in a rural area. My older children ride the bus for almost an hour to the public school. I want my 4-year-old to go to preschool, but I can't take the time to drive her to town. There is no Head Start program in our area, even though we might qualify. The public school does not have a preschool and even if they did, I certainly don't want her riding the bus for an hour with all those older children. What options are there for families like us?

U V Kids do ride together, care for each other.

and effective policies available to improve population health. The CDC (2019) cites a rigorous evidence base for ECE fostering socioemotional, cognitive, and motor skill development, as well as academic achievement. It also points to ECE investment as a way to foster longer-term benefits, such as reductions in obesity, child abuse and neglect, youth violence, teen birth rates, and emergency room visits.

So, how do we move faster and with more intention down this road toward equitable early education? While we have not been able to address all components of Universal Preschool in this book, we focused on research areas from the "Past" and "Present" stories as being the most needed and having the greatest potential for impact.

Shared and Collaborative Leadership

Given the diverse auspices and leadership in early education in the United States, Universal Preschool can exist only through collaboration. Collaboration is elusive, as equity is not static at all levels of power. In other words, one's position of power changes with variables, including culture, point in time, and context. Therefore, it takes intentionality to address assumptions as we engage across power, culture, language, and racial lines. Effective collaborative leadership models include relational and distributed leadership (Chapter 5).

What makes this collaborative policy work worth doing? If early childhood policy is to be responsive to the communities in which it is enacted, collaboration must be redefined as a policy goal. Instead of bringing together communities on the pretense of eliciting their perspectives, efforts must be made to develop the social capital of marginalized groups and document local efforts to make change. When considering successful, participatory partnership structures using negotiated goal setting, Seddon, Billett, and Clemans (2005) suggest that "Such learning means that individuals become more confident, capable and engaged. They create communities that have 'social capital'" (p. 571). This is possible as the relational benefits accrued in daily interactions and planning are shared by the group, rather than fostered individually. While there is not "one way" to create preschool policy, by acknowledging the politics and power of the process, it may be possible through these participatory practices to develop programs that meet the needs of those they serve and avoid the pitfalls of existing archaic formal education systems. Even though there is sufficient literature to support this path, this is not easy work (Burch & Spillane, 2004; Gittell & Douglass, 2012; Good, 2018).

We suggest the merits of pulling from the strength of early educators to honor relationship building—as relationships form a foundational premise in leading collaborative efforts (Gittell & Douglass, 2012). Notions of courageously leading from within, building universal reciprocity, contribute to a collaborative approach that supports networks and social capital toward equitable solutions in early education (Gittell & Douglass, 2012; Palmer, 1994, 2017).

What's in a Name? Universal Preschool

How we define early childhood education plays a big role in moving forward in policies and perceptions in the United States. Currently, Universal Preschool is offered as the most viable solution to the broader educational crisis and, therefore, is receiving increased attention. We find it a bit ironic that even though the pay and support for teachers are lower in ECE than in most other professions, early childhood education is gaining attention as offering hope for the nation.

Through the research and stories in this book, we found defining Universal Preschool problematic, which raised questions regarding equitable investment. Currently, the discourse of Universal Preschool marginalizes the earliest years and conflates preschool with kindergarten. Although not necessarily intentional, this conflation is a real consequence given the powerful discourses in the media.

In order to honor diverse lived experiences, how we envision early education matters. In each step of the policy process, it is crucial to evaluate and assess whose children are affected when writing educational reforms, and how all children receive equity in learning opportunities. We hope our intentional approach to honoring each perspective and experience highlights the need to address the debt to those who currently do not benefit in our educational systems.

Where we focus effort on early education matters. If our efforts exclude children age 3 and under, are we really creating equity for all children and families? For example, the Individuals with Disabilities Act (IDEA) requires that children with disabilities receive services in the least restrictive environment. If Universal Preschool programs are created only for 4-year-old children, what creative public options and funding are available to provide services for any 3-year-olds, much less those with disabilities? Currently, birth-to-3 programming is mandated through IDEA, but if these concerns are not addressed in the universal preschool movement this leaves few options for families with a 3-year-old child with a diagnosed disability. It also misses the mark to support all early childhood programs with resources and serve the needs of *all* young children. Access to equitable education for all children, early in life, facilitates access and equity through the years.

Access and Delivery Models

Multiple formats or models of Universal Preschool programs provide some choice, but also create confusion for families and advocates. The overview in Chapter 3 of one pilot program illustrates four different delivery options, including community centers, family-based care, Head Start, and district sites. Other variables impact how children engage in early learning—issues of licensing, funding streams, profit and nonprofit structures, and mandated curriculum, among others.

These options and variables make the early education net of services difficult for families to untangle. Unless administrators, politicians, educators, and advocates clarify options for families, so they can more easily access funding, services, and support for early education, the net will stay tangled. Delivery models of early education need to fit the unique needs of young children and their families. Policy proposals for funding continue to support school-based models, yet this is just one option. Considering the constant plea for investment in early childhood education and the need for universal access, how can the gaps and frustrations for families be reduced?

Most Universal Preschool programs are sustained primarily with state funds. In 2016, 28% of 4-year-olds were enrolled in state-financed preschools (Barnett et al., 2016). However, cities are starting to increase their investment in local preschool programs as evidence of their effectiveness has mounted. Local investment in preschool is now geographically diverse: Large cities in 15 states across the country now enhance Universal Preschool with local funds (City Health & NIEER, 2019). The diversification of funding sources may provide more freedom for early education models (Committee for Economic Development, 2019; Parker, Diffey, & Atcheson, 2018).

FAMILY PERSPECTIVE

"Sweetie, remember . . . I'll come to school today at lunchtime—that's why you have your PB&J—and we'll eat together. Then I'll show you the bus to get on for Grandma Edie's house so that you can do this all by yourself like the other big girls tomorrow!"

"'kay," Tasha replies with a blank look.

"So for today, I am taking you to Grandma Edie's house, then you'll get on the big bus to school, then I'll see you for lunch, then you'll get back on the bus to Grandma Edie's, and that's where I'll pick you up after work. It will be fine," Mom says, trying to reassure herself as much as Tasha. Flash-forward to Grandma Edie's—Tasha with heels dug in is not willing to get on that big ole bus. She wants to stay with Grandma.

In an overview of recent studies, Barnett, Weisenfeld and colleagues. (2016) concur that high-quality Universal Preschool includes rigorous, articulated, early learning policies with well-educated and well-compensated staff; small class size; full-day offerings; developmentally, culturally, and linguistically appropriate curriculum; inclusive settings for children with a range of abilities; and dual-language support. While this list may seem insurmountable, our stories suggest that it is less about what we craft and more about how we connect and communicate across contexts (agencies, cultures, races, ages) that will define our success in implementing these components for early education.

Investing in support for young children comes in many forms: a community early childhood center, a classroom housed in a public school, or resources offered to families to create relevant home and community educational experiences through relative care or home schooling. By providing the financial support and resources for families to best support their child and the unique needs of their family situation, the likelihood of authentic, and therefore successful, ECE delivery models that address issues of equity is increased.

Standardization and Curriculum

Some would say that we have entered a new era in the experiences available to young children. In Chapter 2, we discussed a key discourse between collaborative partners that revolved around how and what young children learn. We emphasized that young children learn best through hands-on experiences that inspire creativity, experimentation, and problem solving in an atmosphere of trusting and supportive relationships. As discussed in Chapter 1, the intentional practice of incorporating play in early learning environments helps children develop self-regulation—a lifelong skill—and promotes cognition, language skills, and social competence (Nell, Drew, & Bush, 2013). Funding requirements and accountability initiatives may require programs to focus on "school readiness."

With publicly funded programs comes the need to measure the success of implementation—what children are learning and how we can prove it. We are

HEAD START TEACHER PERSPECTIVE

I really loved my job with Head Start, but I just couldn't do it anymore. I decided to take early retirement. I value the time I spend with children and families, but the other requirements were taking so much time! We had many demands on our time to document—there are so many assessments for the children to meet Head Start requirements. I realize we need to ensure that children are making progress in their growth and learning; however, I found I was spending less time with the children and feeling so frustrated. I understand why there are regulations, standards, and accountability; however, it took the joy out of teaching for me.

in somewhat uncharted territory with this requirement in early education. We heard in the Head Start teacher perspective that this discourse can result in the loss of dedicated and highly qualified teachers. Translating authentic assessment strategies such as work sampling and documentation to connect across educational contexts is possible but challenging. Decades of research suggest that playful learning involves pedagogical tools through which young children learn in conceptually rich and joyful ways (Masterson & Bohart, 2019). And yet, packaged curricula and teacher-directed practices do not always inspire playful learning.

Young children require pedagogical flexibility from teachers, administrators, and program mandates. The current trend toward shifting learning standards from K–12 settings to younger populations fails to honor the increased range of growth and development happening in the early years; it excludes populations of learners. Standardized approaches fail to allow for flexibility to engage children in ways that honor cultural and linguistic needs (Darling-Hammond, 2015; Ravitch, 2016).

Early childhood teachers are under pressure to prepare young children for a standardized formal school situation while simultaneously meeting individual, cultural, and sociopolitical needs (Brown, 2015). This pressure is taking a toll on all stakeholders. Rather than pushing a standardized system down and creating "a new kindergarten" with 3- and 4-year-olds, we call for consideration of early education pedagogical strategies in the primary grades of the K–12 system.

Addressing the Education Debt and Honoring Home Language

Nationwide, students who are dual-language learners constitute about 23% of the preschool-age population. Dual-language learners live in every state. Yet, most state preschool programs do not collect data on children's home language (Barnett, Yarosz, Thomas, Jung, & Blanco, 2007). This lack of data impedes policy development and implementation to support effective classroom practices to meet diverse linguistic needs. Qualified teachers who linguistically, culturally, and racially represent those they are teaching are key to providing high-quality early learning experiences that prepare young children for later school and life success.

Too often, the strengths of student learning in more than one language, or of students bringing a different cultural perspective, are overlooked due to universal standard measures. One way of addressing the pedagogical disconnection between standardization and early education is through shifting approaches from an achievement gap based on standard notions of achievement to an education debt. This allows closer examination of the deeper issues connected to curricula. Ladson-Billings (2006) calls out the need to consider the "historical, economic, socio-political and moral components" (p. 3) of an education debt, rather than continue to focus on the achievement gap based on standardized testing. "Rather than focus solely on students' failures to 'measure up' to universal academic standards, the conversation must address the efficacy of curricula to be implemented across diverse contexts" (Michael-Luna, Heimer, & Grey, 2020, p. 122). This shifts the onus for the achievement gap off the child (and teachers) and provides rationale for education policy reform to address a debt owed to the child.

Darling-Hammond (2015) suggests the need for new approaches in education to address the "opportunity gap." This gap is not new and continues to widen and evolve as equity issues regarding access to quality education continue to pose a societal dilemma. Equity for children and families is implied by the term *universal*, and although efforts are being made, there is a renewed sense of urgency in our communities as we see disparate proficiency levels continue. In putting equity at the center of the process, we suggest:

1. Measured use of global terms (e.g., UPK)
2. Awareness of the paradox of collaboration
3. Avoidance of overemphasis on standardization of curriculum
4. Recognition of the education debt

With these cautions in mind, the next steps for investment in early childhood education will be more intentional. In our final "Present" story, teachers' critical inquiry and reflection impact the daily implementation of Universal Preschool policy.

PRESENT STORY: NYC PRE-K FOR ALL—CONFLICTING INTERESTS AND BELIEFS AROUND CURRICULUM AND ASSESSMENT

Lacey Peters

Pre-K for All (PKFA) is the name of New York City's universalized prekindergarten program. New York City has had a Universal Pre-K program since 1997. But the city experienced a broad expansion starting in 2014, when the current mayor, Bill de Blasio, was elected. Mayor de Blasio prioritized early care and education and called on city agencies to increase the number of pre-K classrooms so that more than 70,000 children and their families could have access to free, high-quality pre-K programming. In addition to addressing the issue of accessibility, policymakers and other stakeholders placed a heavy emphasis on program quality. Due to the large investment of public funding in pre-K programs, there are heightened accountability and quality control measures for teachers and instructional leaders. For example, the Department of Education (DOE) set a mandate for teachers to use one of three assessment systems: My Teaching Strategies, the Work Sampling System, or High Scope's Child Observation Record. In addition, the DOE created "Interdisciplinary Units of Study" for teachers to follow. The extent to which teachers use the Units of Study varies, but it is not uncommon to see teachers in different programs teaching similar topics and engaging children in similar activities at the same time. Teachers also are expected to attend professional learning workshops around different topics related to social–emotional learning, early childhood math, creative arts, inquiry-based learning, and data-driven instruction. The initiatives around curriculum and assessment are intended to help teachers improve their practice, and seek to create consistency across sites so that children and families have similar experiences during pre-K, no matter where they go. These initiatives also reinforce the accountability measures used to evaluate program quality, teaching effectiveness, and child outcomes.

Colleagues and I have been working on a research project in PKFA programs since 2016 and have captured the perspectives of teachers, educational directors, and parents of 4-year-old children as the pre-K expansion has transpired. We situate much of our work within a critical ecology of the early childhood profession framework (Dalli, Miller, & Urban, 2012) to give deeper meaning to the teachers' professional lived experiences. Following the critical ecology approach, teachers are encouraged to transform practices and policies within systems through critical reflection, inquiry, and responsiveness in their local contexts. In order to engage teachers in critical inquiry, one must first understand teachers' ways of knowing and ways of being practical.

During the 2016–2017 school year, we worked very closely with 14 Pre-K for All teachers, all but two of whom worked in community-based organizations (CBOs). The programs or schools were located in neighborhoods that ranged from low-, to moderate-, to high-resource levels across the boroughs of the Bronx, Brooklyn, and Manhattan. The women we worked with were of diverse cultural and racial backgrounds and identified as Black or African American, White, Latina, and mixed race. They each held different levels of teaching experience ranging from less than 1 year to more than 20 years in a classroom. Several of the teachers had experience using authentic assessment systems, yet for others, the 2016–2017 school year provided their first opportunity to use authentic assessment. The children and families in their classrooms were also of diverse cultural and linguistic backgrounds.

The primary focus of our project was authentic assessment, and we were interested in learning about how teachers use authentic assessment systems to inform their pedagogical decisionmaking and to communicate with family members about children's growth and learning. Yet, because of the timing and phenomenological nature of our study, we have come to learn a great deal about their experiences adapting to the new requirements and expectations for curriculum and instruction. Among the things we are learning is how teachers' pedagogical decisionmaking is being shaped by the mechanisms used to determine quality and how the teachers have influence over their daily lived experiences in classrooms, such as the mandate to use authentic assessment. Teachers encounter tensions or experience a push-and-pull between deciding how to approach their work based on their knowledge, experiences, and expertise, and following the recommended practices endorsed or set by other people.

Regardless of teachers' beliefs about systems like Teaching Strategies GOLD, they don't have a choice in deciding whether to use them or not. As previously stated, this is a mandate to ensure that teachers actually are carrying out an approved form of assessment; additionally, they are required to submit their assessment data to the DOE three times a year. At this point, teachers are concerned with meeting the expectations set by the DOE in order to keep their jobs. The heightened accountability fosters a culture of compliance, which in turn is shifting the roles and responsibilities of early childhood professionals working on the ground, and the opportunities for them to be critically engaged in their work are limited. The question then emerges: What are the possibilities for teachers to transform practices and policies within the system if they do not agree with the mandates?

Fortunately, policymakers and people working with, or for, all city agencies continuously are seeking ways to improve systems of pre-K education, including revising policies and making changes to programming and recommended practices. As these decisions are made, we think it is vital for teachers to be a part of the conversation. Teachers across all levels of education are facing increased pressure to conform to standardization or prescribed approaches to curriculum and teaching. In early childhood, academically oriented definitions of kindergarten readiness, in combination with the "accountability shovedown" (Hatch, 2002a), are restructuring preschool and prekindergarten experiences for teachers, children, and families. As the early childhood landscape continues to transform, and while the system of pre-K education grows over time, we will continue to pay close attention to teachers' voices and daily classroom experiences in order to advocate for teachers' agency and influence in decisions made for or about their professional lives. Our vision is (1) that this research will turn into action, and consequently teachers will embody a greater sense of empowerment as they realize people are listening and they are being heard; and (2) that ultimately engagement in critical inquiry and reflection around their teaching will become an embedded practice, whether it is related to assessment, curriculum, family partnerships, community building, or culturally responsive pedagogies or not.

SUMMARY: KEEPING WONDER AT THE HEART OF WISDOM

We started this chapter reflecting on the path of powerful insights to consider what is possible in early childhood education and what the ECE system "might become." Keeping the wonder alive, we continue to advocate for early childhood systems that nurture equity, leadership, and intentional collaboration.

The insights across 15 years of Universal Preschool policy through "Past" and "Present" stories and perspectives have provided a partial road map. Use of critical theory, centering on the experiences of participants, illuminates the strengths and barriers, and validates the need to consider diverse perspectives.

We offer both an urgent and cautious call to collaborate across varied existing early education contexts. This caution applies at the national and state levels, where all too often the effects of a fragmented ECE system are not understood. Expansion funds are allocated or new programs are started without connections to existing programs and services. At the local level, where the practical application of offering collaborative ECE services plays out, conscious approaches to collaboration are key. At all levels, equity in all phases of collaboration and implementation is required.

Issues of access to equitable education in the United States remain across all developmental levels. Early childhood education falls under different auspices and too often is marginalized within larger educational systems, and yet may offer key insights leading to stronger programming across public and private sectors. While there are many initiatives in ECE, they can be confusing to families and the general public.

The need to standardize the early childhood profession (with higher credentials and packaged curriculum), along with the reality of low pay, creates a dilemma. The call for more access to Universal Preschool is prevalent; however, the resources to answer this call are lacking. The stories in this book offer hope as families and teachers gain traction toward autonomy with equity through critical reflection, academic connection, and political initiatives. The arguments for societal investment in early education remain:

- From a neuroscience standpoint, the early years matter.
- From an economic standpoint, the early years matter.
- From an equity lens, the early years matter!

In treating early education as a national priority, we can begin to pay the education debt by investing early in creative ways for all children.

REFLECTIVE CONVERSATIONS AND ACTIONS

1. In this book we join the synergy of wonder to the practicality of wisdom to navigate complicated systems of power, relationships, and discourse.
   - Where can you insert wonder into your thoughts, conversations, and actions around Universal Preschool efforts?
   - How can you honor the wisdom of all families and individuals? Possible resources: National Equity Project: nationalequityproject.org/resources
2. "So what happens in 3rd grade? The kid [of color] has been taught that they are the problem and they start to shut down," says Hibbler, who is Black. "By 6th grade they are labeled 'monster' and disengage even more. By the time the kid is in high school, they have years of negative interactions in schools and are years behind academically." Hibbler is

critical of the top-down leadership. . . . He says teachers need to be held accountable but systemic racism can't be solved in one classroom. "Believe me, I've tried," says Hibbler. "That's why every teacher needs to practice equity and exercise compassion from the very beginning. Kids see that and flock to it" (Brogan, 2019). How does the quote connect to the Universal Preschool movement? How might the issue of race open up the possibilities for early education in the United States?

3. How can the results from the CDC on the benefits of Universal Preschool (i.e., positive health impacts, long-term gains in a short period, and cost-effectiveness) provide powerful persuasive points in our discussions with others? Based on the "Past" and "Present" stories of this text, how might we frame these findings to caution against a one-size-fits-all approach and offer equitable access to honor all children and families?

4. What can you do in your current role as an early childhood professional, parent, grandparent, or community member to participate in Universal Preschool discussions, planning, or implementation? Why should you do so?

5. Compose an editorial piece on Universal Preschool for your local paper. What would you write? What research would you use? How would you provide a balanced argument that might invite collaborative nods rather than reactive division?

Conclusion

We enter the world in a state of wonder. Quickly immersed in a variety of contexts, the wonder becomes framed and channeled in particular ways. As a society, we have an opportunity to consider how to craft approaches to respect that initial wonder possessed by all children, as it is nested in home contexts, offering valuable and diverse strengths. These strengths include culture, language, and ways of being that are experienced by the child as "home." In early education, we have a responsibility to honor the strength of the home influence by creating plans, policies, and programs inclusive of these ways of being.

Now is the time to create plans in early education that are funded in new ways, engage children in respectful authentic contexts, and build pathways founded on the wisdom in the wonder. Using critical approaches, we have explored the potential and possibilities of collaborative Universal Preschool as one creative approach. We have critiqued the use of terminology that lumps early education in with formal K–12 systems. And we have suggested consideration for how, as a nation, we define and label early education as a unique, but related, system of support for families and children—from birth onward. There are many aspects of early education systems and practices that offer insights on ways to strengthen K–12 education: (a) the strengths of relationship-based approaches, (b) meeting the individual needs of children, and (c) offering an array of education options and settings for families. What can the K–12 system learn from early childhood? How can the K–12 system honor the importance of the early childhood system? We propose that both systems work together to create powerful new approaches for learning, keeping the best of both worlds, to the benefit of children and families.

As we shared in the Preface, how we define "universal" is key. The stories from research, coupled with published evidence, suggest that investing creativity, time, and resources in children and families is a required next step to address larger educational needs in the United States. However, we have questioned the Universal Preschool movement as a panacea and have shared stories that acknowledge the "debt" or inequity inherent in universal approaches. As we enact broad sweeping policy, it is imperative to consider the multiple perspectives in order to continue the conversation beyond access to equity. There is an urgent need to provide support for and access to early education, including Universal Preschool. How we carefully and intentionally take the next steps is the question that must be steeped in wonder and wisdom.

"Circles" by Ann Elizabeth Ramminger

Deep are the roots, in the circle of life
trees and children, reach for the sky ...
Stars twinkling, children circle round

Conversations are held, with hands on cups,
tables are round, and so are the cookies ...
In the soft warm sand, children draw circles

How many hands, are touching the wheel
when sailing the ship, into the future ...
Going round and round, children hold hands

The planets align, as wonder abides
Wisdom reigns, for the stars of the future ...
Searching our faces, children have hope

Interlocking

Image: Lucinda Grace Heimer

Methodology

RESEARCH QUESTIONS

The original research provided data for the "Past" UPK stories and explored how the needs of young children in one Midwestern state were addressed through a collaborative policy movement, the Early Childhood Collaborative, and the UPK pilot program. This instrumental case study (Stake, 1995) looked at one school district's efforts to implement UPK. The research questions were:

- How do notions of collaboration get enacted in policy creation and implementation of a pilot kindergarten program for 4-year-olds?
- Who is invited and able to participate in policy creation?
- How does the leadership of this 4K collaboration function?
- How are memory and politics related in the retelling(s) of the ECC story(ies)?
- What were the costs and benefits in this case in terms of creating a "universal" approach?

CONTEXT OF THE ECC

During the ECC policy formulation stage (Rist, 1998), observations took place primarily in policy meetings (March 2001–March 2003). Specifically, the policy formulation phase consisted of school district board meetings, committee meetings, public forums, and informal lunches. I (Lucinda) met with participants in key meetings, public forums, and individually. Meetings took place in United Way buildings, Head Start sites, a corporate office, child-care centers, and school district administrative offices. Meeting attendance shifted over the course of the project (see Chapter 3) and included early care and education, district, and Head Start administrators, and child advocacy and referral agency staff. The meetings occurred from once a month to once a week as needs shifted. Most meetings occurred during the work week and generally lasted 2 hours. This stage of the process was fairly visible in the media from September 2002 to May 2003, as the local paper ran a series on early childhood education issues in the community. Following the ECC policy formulation stage and the subsequent tabling of the initiative, the focus of the research shifted to the UPK pilot (March 2003).

UPK PILOT

The UPK pilot portion of the research encompassed both policy formulation and implementation, with details of the policy to be determined separately. The initial observations (March 2003–August 2003) during the policy formulation stage were held mostly at Greentree Elementary or Abbott Center at the university and research offices. The participants included the university research team, a university child-care director, school administrators, Head Start administrators, district early childhood specialist, other researchers, and a city office of outreach services representative (not a complete list).

During the implementation stage, I worked in the classrooms of the pilot UPK program. There were two classrooms: one at the Head Start site (Waterfront) and one at a public elementary school (Greentree). In terms of Arborville's demographics, both sites were located in diverse (racially and economically) neighborhoods. The pilot sites were approximately 2 miles from each other and shared school attendance areas. However, the Head Start site was located in a converted duplex on the same block as many of the housing units in a lower-resourced area. Many of the children living in these units attended the Head Start site. The classroom in Greentree was located on the lower level of the elementary school, next to the cafeteria, and across from the early childhood program for children with special needs. Each classroom had 14 to 17 children, with one teacher and one assistant. The Head Start site served one group of children with a morning session only, while the Greentree site had both morning and afternoon sessions. During the 2003–2004 school year, I visited classrooms as a participant/observer, conducting interviews, compiling fieldnotes, and collecting artifacts.

ROLE OF THE RESEARCHER

For the original research used in the "Past" UPK stories, my primary role was researcher. However, positions held in the past (teacher, director, student) influenced observations of teachers and leaders. As a research assistant on a related project, in August 2003, an additional focus of mine included academic outcomes for children involved in the 4K pilot program. From August 2003 to July 2004, data collection for academic outcomes continued, as well as collection of data for the original research. Throughout the course of the research, a dilemma surfaced involving how to present the data, as I had a position of power and privilege over its interpretation (Britzman, 1991; Lather, 1991). As narrator, the goal was to recount the teachers' experiences, not unlike the role a discussant might play for a presentation panel. The process included reviewing their stories; assessing insights, strengths, and context; and informing larger research questions.

Keeping in mind that the researcher and the "researched" both were situated historically, socially, and culturally (Graue & Walsh, 1998), recognizing my subjectivity versus objectivity was a crucial part of the role of researcher (Peshkin, 1988). Considerations included how information was interpreted, whose story was told, and what purposes were served through the stories (Beck et al., 2001). The insights and connections to the early childhood network in this district provided a "big picture" beyond the classroom; yet questions arose regarding other aspects of my experience, including my roles as practitioner and researcher, the expertise that I brought to the process, and my interest in specific areas of the research.

At a literal level, the policy creation phase was initiated while I was working in the field. Previously established relationships with research participants brought complexity to the project. Conversely, the context and my participation in the classroom represented new territory for me. During the initial research, there was a delicate balance of gaining social capital and access to informal networks of information, while still building relationships with new participants (primarily the teachers). My involvement in classrooms, and eventually writing collaboratively with one of the teachers, provided a richness of information that is expressed in this book. Finally, as my personal life shifted and a new role as parent emerged, perspectives on the impacts of programming for families sharpened.

The role of researcher as storyteller emerged to navigate the complex nature of subjectivity/objectivity. Telling the stories of the ECC and UPK pilot, while researching the meaning and function of collaboration, became the research path. The "Past" UPK stories are told from the researcher perspective at the time of occurrence. It is acknowledged that these stories might be different if they were written during other parts of the researcher's professional career.

Informed consent was obtained from all participants in the study. Ongoing consent was required for children. Each family and child had rights and options, at any time, to opt out of interviewing or interacting in individual, small, or large groups for research purposes. It was a family decision to participate when and if they were comfortable, and all research activities (interviews, one-on-one sharing in the classroom, etc.) were optional.

DATA COLLECTION

For both policy formulation and implementation stages of the policy process, data collection methods included participant observation and participant/researcher communication (Corsaro & Molinari, 2000; Graue & Walsh, 1998), semistructured interviews, and document analysis (Hodder, 1998). With a focus on power (specifically in terms of discourse and relationships), these methods served to provide context for a pluralistic analytical process.

Participant Observation

There was a dual purpose of participant observation: that of observing but also participating in the classroom. However, there was an explicit awareness that the purpose was to gather research data. The key to use of this type of collection technique was awareness of the focus of the observation in relation to the question being asked (Graue & Walsh, 1998). Although there were multiple interactions and areas of interest in the classroom for my research, my focus was on the observation of the interpretation and implementation of the 4K policies. Classrooms were observed naturalistically, on average twice a week, as I functioned as a research assistant and aide in the classroom: at Head Start two mornings a week during fall 2003 and one morning a week during spring 2004; and at the Greentree classroom two afternoons a week in fall 2003 and one afternoon a week in spring 2004.

A general format for fieldnotes was used when "cooking" my fieldnotes. Observations were recorded through participant observation fieldnotes, which were analyzed interpretively and used to describe the nature of (1) instructional activities (including format, content, pedagogy, and social relations); (2) experience of the children (as expressed through children's choices made in class, peer interactions, artwork shared, small- and large-group interactions and informal conversations); (3) environment; and (4) nature of events present in the UPK program (parent events, conferences, registration, classroom volunteering etc.). Analysis of observations took into consideration how the experiences related to the discourses and contextual framings mentioned earlier (universal access and collaboration). For example, small meetings that provided insight into informal collaboration were scheduled throughout the day. My participation in the classroom allowed movement beyond the statistics of classroom composition to consider alternative meanings and implications of universal access. As my role shifted my level of participation also shifted, allowing more time in the classroom the first semester. The initial focus on classroom practices helped create familiarity for the children, as I took an active role in small groups and other teaching activities. By teaching and being involved in staff meetings, I had access to a wide range of information, which I documented. As a complement to the participant/observer data, interviews were conducted with multiple participants.

Interviewing

Working with a community perspective in mind, and with the understanding that multiple sites of knowledge exist within those participating, I used a semistructured and informal structure for interviewing. There was continued conscious awareness that the interviewer (knowingly or not) inevitably can influence the process. Therefore, there was concerted emphasis on the role of the interviewee, and I limited my role as researcher in the process (Fontana & Frey, 1998).

I conducted interviews with teachers (two teachers; six interviews), social workers (two social workers; four interviews), and administrators (six administrators; six interviews), using the semistructured interview format (Graue & Walsh, 1998). In addition, the child interviews took the form of a small-group activity with the children (three total at Head Start and five total at Greentree—decided by the interests of the children).

The semistructured interview allowed for well-formulated, purposeful questions, yet also allowed for flexibility to probe further or allow the interviewee to expound if appropriate. Spradley (1980) suggests that questions and answers during an ethnographic interview are discovered from informants. As researcher, I inevitably influenced the participants; however, through the analysis process, I worked to address perceived power in the process and provide access to the multiple stories they shared. Transcribed interviews were available to all participants. The teachers provided feedback on what was used for the research, primarily for Chapter 5.

The questions in all interviews were geared toward better understanding the involvement of participants in the policy process and their subsequent interpretations of the ECC and 4K pilot. Participants were reminded of their choice to opt out of any question or the process itself. Interviews were taped, transcribed, and analyzed thematically in relation to classroom observations and other artifacts.

Artifact Analysis

Finally, throughout I used document analysis and collected artifacts (Hatch, 2002b; Hodder, 1998), including:

- Parent questionnaires
- Lesson plans
- Meeting minutes
- Newspaper articles
- Public relations videos
- Child assessment results (including the Child Assessment Profile, Woodcock-Johnson III, and the Social Skills Rating Scale)
- An Early Language and Literacy Classroom Observation (ELLCO)
- Children's work
- Parent letters
- Photographs of classrooms
- Policy manuals
- Curriculum guides

These artifacts were copied, organized, and placed in binders to represent Greentree and Head Start sites. Teachers and participants were informed at the onset of the project of my interest to collect these data and the value of these items to create a thicker description was stressed. Using this analysis, I considered the value of artifacts in relation to other data. Whenever possible, I tried to quote texts directly and provide other contextual information.

All of the data gathered, the interactions involved in the process, and the contexts (historical, cultural, political, social) influenced not only the data collection process but also the materials used in the process. I connected concepts and ideas, from formulation to enactment of policy, through the triangulation of data (voices, actions, and artifacts of those involved).

Sampling

Initially, I attempted to attend every related event, forum, training, meeting, and activity during the policy formulation process (2001–2003), while also striving to maintain relationships with key participants, including administrators, children, teachers, families, community members, and other researchers. With the increased number of research participants and contexts, a shift was made to sampling. Spradley (1980) suggests sampling not just participants but events, settings, and processes. This is considered "combination sampling" (Hatch, 2002b), looking at both typical and politically purposeful cases.

Sampling Participants. For each phase of the process, I considered the gatekeepers for access to the program (Hatch, 2002b). To facilitate access, I cultivated professional relationships with many of the gatekeepers: the director and assistant director of Head Start, the principal of the school, the director of the ECC initiative, and university researchers. The following individuals were participants in the project either through observations, questionnaires, or interviews:

District administrators: Lead elementary principal for the district and
   district consultant
Community members: Director of city office of outreach services and
   director of Head Start
University community members: University researcher and director of
   university child-care services
Teachers: Greentree Elementary and Waterfront Head Start
Social workers: Greentree Elementary and Waterfront Head Start
All children and families at each site: Approximately 43 children and
   their families

Administrators and community members were chosen for interviews based on length of time involved in the process, level of responsibility, and/or power in the community regarding the initiative.

Sampling Events. As Spradley (1980) suggests, sampling also includes events; therefore, I selected events and meetings that offered a cross-section of experiences: family nights, registration with families, planning meetings with staff, staff meetings, policy evaluation meetings, early childhood community meetings, and so on. It was not possible to attend every meeting or event, so some meetings were attended initially, to establish myself as researcher and resource. Given the large number of participants and events, the use of sampling allowed time to stay current with data collection and notes.

DATA ANALYSIS

Initially, I reviewed the data and began to look for patterns within the data sets. Use of memos and coding as techniques helped organize thoughts in relation to the emerging themes. The codes assisted in identifying themes in various chunks of data. I took into consideration the role of both internal (my reading of the data) and external (theoretically based) coding influences (Graue & Walsh, 1998). Questions to help focus on the process, rather than the outcome, of analysis included:

- What are people doing? What are they trying to accomplish?
- How exactly do they do this? What specific means and/or strategies do they use?
- How do members talk about, characterize, and understand what is going on?
- What assumptions are they making?
- What do I see going on here? What did I learn from these notes?
- Why did I include them? (Emerson, Fretz, & Shaw, 1995, p. 146)

Although the coding started with categories, such as collaboration, universal access/diversity, policy, and curriculum, subdivided by classroom (parents, teachers, staff, children), agency (public school, Head Start, university, etc.), and interactions between these entities, those categories soon were refined into new coding categories. Collaboration became the overarching coded discourse, and within this, separate categories emerged for administrators, teachers, social workers, families, and children in terms of: enrollment, definition and interpretation of curriculum, agency policy influences, leadership, participant access, staff perceptions of families, and language. From these codes, extensive memos were created that allowed integration of theoretical perspectives in relation to the patterns emerging. As I reviewed the memos, themes emerged and stories were grouped accordingly. For example, in Chapter 5, although leadership was a central focus, the stories of curriculum and agency policy influences helped define what was happening in the classrooms. Although I recognized that many of these codes, memos, and themes overlapped, the book was compiled in a way that would be most useful in terms of analyzing a collaborative policy initiative. Wherever possible, I used quotes from participants to reflect their word choice in explaining their experience. In addition, I used vignettes to supplement the data and provide examples of what the process looked like as it occurred (Graue & Walsh, 1998). Throughout the research and writing process, I understood that it was through my choosing and interpretation that the themes were expanded for further research.

References

Abowitz, K. (2003). Civil society and educational publics. In G. Dimitriades & D. Carlson (Eds.), *Promises to keep: Cultural studies, democratic education and public life* (pp. 77–94). New York, NY: Routledge.

Allen, K. E., Bordas, J., Hickman, G. R., Matusak, L. R., Sorenson, G. J., & Whitmire, K. J. (1997). *Leadership in the 21st century.* Kellogg Foundation Report. Retrieved from kathleenallen.net/wp-content/uploads/2017/12/Leadership-in-the-Twenty-First-Century.pdf

Apple, M. W. (2018). *The struggle for democracy in education.* New York, NY: Routledge.

Arborville School District. (2002, December 9). Board meeting packet.

Arts Consulting Group. (2003). *Insights: Strategic collaborations, 3*(9). Retrieved from artsconsulting.com/arts-insights/arts-insights-archive/

Au, W., & Ferrare, J. J. (2015). *Mapping corporate education reform: Power and policy networks in the neoliberal state.* New York, NY: Routledge.

Bailey, D., Duncan, G. J., Odgers, C. L., & Yu, W. (2017). Persistence and fadeout in the impacts of child and adolescent interventions. *Journal of Research on Educational Effectiveness, 10*(1), 7–39. doi:10.1080/19345747.2016.1232459

Baldwin, J. (1963). A talk to teachers. *The Saturday Review, 44*(28), 42–44.

Baldwin, J. (2011, April 12). The crusade of indignation. *The Nation.* (Original work published July 7, 1956) Retrieved from www.thenation.com/article/crusade-indignation/

Ball, S. (1994). *Education reform: A critical and post-structural approach.* Buckingham, UK: Open University Press.

Barnett, W. S. (2010). Universal and targeted approaches to preschool education in the United States. *International Journal of Child Care and Education Policy, 4*(1), 1–12.

Barnett, W. S., Brown, K., & Shore, R. (2004). *The universal vs. targeted debate: Should the United States have preschool for all?* (Policy Brief, Issue 6). New Brunswick, NJ: National Institute for Early Education Research. Retrieved from nieer.org/wp-content/uploads/2016/08/6.pdf

Barnett, W. S., Friedman-Krauss, A. H., Weisenfeld, G. G., Horowitz, M., Kasmin, R., & Squires, J. H. (2017). *The state of preschool 2016.* Retrieved from nieer.org/wp-content/uploads/2017/08/Executive-Summary_8.21.17.pdf

Barnett, W. S., & Gomez, R. E. (2016). *Universal pre-K: What does it mean and who provides it?* New Brunswick, NJ: National Institute for Early Education Research.

Barnett, W. S., & Kasmin, R. (2017). *Teacher compensation parity policies and state-funded pre-K programs.* New Brunswick, NJ: National Institute for Early Education Research & Berkeley, California: Center for the Study of Child Care Employment, University of California, Berkeley.

Barnett, W. S., & Kasmin, R. (2018). Fully funding pre-K through K–12 funding formulas. *State Education Standard, 18*(1), 22–28.

Barnett, W. S., Robin, K. B., Hustedt, J. T., & Schulman, K. L. (2003). *The state of preschool. 2003 state preschool yearbook.* New Brunswick, NJ: Rutgers University, The National Institute for Early Education Research.

Barnett, W. S., Weisenfeld, G. G., Brown, K. C., Squires, J., & Horowitz, M. (2016). *Implementing 15 essential elements for high quality: A state and local policy scan.* New Brunswick, NJ: National Institute for Early Education Research & Berkeley, CA: Center for the Study of Child Care.

Barnett, W. S., Yarosz, D. J., Thomas, J., Jung, K., & Blanco, D. (2007). Two-way and monolingual English immersion in preschool education: An experimental comparison. *Early Childhood Research Quarterly, 22*(3), 277–293.

Two-Way and Monolingual English Immersion in Preschool Education: An Experimental Comparison, Early Childhood Research Quarterly, v22 n3 p277-293 Beatty, B. (1995). *Preschool education in America: The culture of young children from the colonial era to the present.* New Haven, CT: Yale University Press.

Beatty, B. (2012). Rethinking compensatory education: Historical perspectives on race, class, culture, language, and the discourse of the "disadvantaged child." *Teachers College Record, 114*(6), 1–11.

Beck, C., DuPont, L., Geismar-Ryan, L., Henke, L., Mitchell Pierce, K., & Von Hatten, C. (2001). Who owns the story? Ethical issues in the conduct of practitioner research. In J. Zeni (Ed.), *Ethical Issues in Practitioner Research.* New York, NY: Teachers College Press.

Becker, K., & Mastrangelo, S. (2017). Ontario's early learning–kindergarten program. *Young Children, 72*(4), 17–23.

Bell, D. (1987). *And we are not saved: The elusive quest for racial justice.* New York, NY: Basic Books.

Berk, L. E., & Winsler, A. (1995). *Scaffolding children's learning: Vygotsky and early childhood education.* Washington, DC: National Association for the Education of Young Children.

Berliner, D. (2006). Our impoverished view of educational reform. *Teachers College Record, 108*(6), pp. 949–995. Retrieved from www.tcrecord.org/content.asp?contentid=12106

Berner, A. R. (2016). *Pluralism and American public education: No one way to school.* New York, NY: Palgrave Macmillan.

Bloch, M., Swadener, B. B., & Cannella, G. S. (2014). *Reconceptualizing early childhood care and education: Critical questions, new imaginaries and social activism.* New York, NY: Peter Lang.

Bodrova, E., & Leong, D. J. (2007). *Tools of the mind: The Vygotskian approach to early childhood education* (2nd ed.). NJ: Pearson.

Bouffard, S. (2017). *The most important year: Pre-kindergarten and the future of our children.* New York, NY: Avery.

Bourdieu, P. (1977). *Outline of a theory of practice.* New York, NY: Cambridge University Press.

Bourdieu, P. (1984). *Distinction: The social critique of the judgement of taste.* Cambridge, MA: Harvard University Press.

Bourdieu, P. (1986). The forms of capital. In J. G. Richardson (Ed.), *Handbook of theory and research for the sociology of education* (pp. 241–258). New York, NY: Greenwood Press.

Bourdieu, P. (1989). Social space and symbolic power. *Sociological Theory, 7*(1), 14–25. Retrieved from http://dx.doi.org/10.2307/20206

Bourdieu, P. (2000). *Pascalian meditations.* Stanford, CA: Stanford University Press.

Bourdieu, P., & Wacquant, L. (1992). *An invitation to reflexive sociology.* Chicago, IL: University of Chicago Press.

Bredekamp, S., Knuth, R. A., Kunesh, L. G., & Shulman, D. D. (1992). *What does research say about early childhood education?* Oakbrook, IL: North Central Regional Educational Laboratory.

Britzman, D. (1991). *Practice makes practice.* Albany, NY: State University of New York Press.

Brogan, D. (2019, May 16). A rotten year. Retrieved from isthmus.com/news/coverstory/rotten-year/

Brown, C. P. (2007). Unpacking standards in early childhood education. *Teachers College Record, 109*(3), 635–668.

Brown, C. P. (2015). Conforming to reform: Teaching pre-kindergarten in a neoliberal early education system. *Journal of Early Childhood Research, 13*(3), 236–251.

Brown, C. P., & Gasko, J. W. (2012). Why should pre-K be more like elementary school: A case of pre-K reform. *Journal of Research in Childhood Education, 26*, 264–290.

Brown C. P., & Lan, Y. (2015). A qualitative metasynthesis of how early educators in international contexts address cultural matters that contrast with developmentally appropriate practices, *Early Education and Development, 26*(1), 22–45. doi:10 .1080/10409289.2014.934176

Brown, C. P., Mowry, B., & Feger, B. (2015). Helping others understand academic rigor in teachers' developmentally appropriate practices. *Young Children, 70*(4), 62–69.

Brown, J. (2007). *A leader's guide to reflective practice.* Victoria, BC: Trafford Publishing.

Buffet Early Childhood Institute. (2013). Strategic master plan. Retrieved from https://buffettinstitute.nebraska.edu/-/media/beci/docs/buffett-institute-strategic-master-plan.pdf?la=en

Burch, P., & Spillane, J. (2004). *Leading from the middle: Mid-level district staff and instructional improvement.* Chicago, IL: Cross City Campaign for Urban School Reform. Retrieved from www.issuelab.org/resources/11963/11963.pdf

Cannella G. S., & Viruru, R. (2004). *Childhood and postcolonization: Power, education and contemporary practice.* New York, NY: Routledge.

Capizzano, J., & Adams, G. (2004). Children in low-income families are less likely to be in center-based child care. *Snapshots of America's Families III., *(16). Washington, DC: The Urban Institute. Retrieved from www.urban.org/Uploaded-PDF/310923_snapshots3_no16.pdf

Casto, H. G., Sipple, J. W., & McCabe, L. A. (2014). A typology of school–community relationships: Partnering and universal prekindergarten policy. *Educational Policy, 30*(5), 659–687. doi.org/10.1177/0895904814557770

Center on the Developing Child. (2011, February). *Building the brain's "air traffic control" system: How early experiences shape the development of executive function* (Working paper). Cambridge, MA: Center on the Developing Child, Harvard University.

Centers for Disease Control and Prevention (CDC). (2019, May 22). Early childhood education: Health impact in five years (HI-5). Retrieved from www.cdc.gov/policy/hst/hi5/interventions/

Choi, J. Y., Elicker, J., Christ, S., & Dobbs-Oates, J. (2016). Predicting growth trajectories in early academic learning: Evidence from growth curve modeling with Head Start children. *Early Childhood Research Quarterly, 36*(3), 244–258. doi:10.1016/j.ecresq.2015.12.017

Chrislip, D. (2002). *The collaborative leadership fieldbook.* San Francisco, CA: Jossey-Bass.

Christakis, E. (2016). *The importance of being little: What young children really need from grownups.* New York, NY: Penguin Books.

City for All Women Initiative. (2015). *Advancing equity and inclusion: A guide for municipalities.* Retrieved from www.cawi-ivtf.org/sites/default/files/publications/advancing-equity-inclusion-web.pdf

City Health & NIEER. (2019, June 22). *Pre-K in American cities.* Retrieved from nieer.org/wp-content/uploads/2019/01/Pre-K-Report-Final.pdf

Committee for Economic Development, Research and Policy Committee. (2002). *Preschool for all: Investing in a productive and just society.* Retrieved from www.ced.org/reports/single/preschool-for-all-investing-in-a-productive-and-just-society

Committee for Economic Development. (2019). Child care in state economies—2019 update. Retrieved from www.ced.org/childcareimpact

Copple, C., & Bredekamp, S. (2009). *Developmentally appropriate practice in early childhood programs serving children from birth through age 8.* Washington, DC: National Association for the Education of Young Children.

Corsaro, W. A., & Molinari, L. (2000). Entering and observing in children's worlds: A reflection on a longitudinal ethnography of early education in Italy. In P. Christensen & A. James (Eds.), *Research with children: Perspectives and practices,* (pp. 239–259). London, UK: Routledge/Falmer.

Dalli, C., Miller, L., & Urban, M. (2012). Early childhood grows up: Towards a critical ecology of the profession. In C. Dalli, L. Miller, & M. Urban (Eds.), *Early childhood grows up Towards a critical ecology of the profession* (pp. 3–19). Dordrecht, Netherlands: Springer.

Darling-Hammond, L. (2015). *The flat world and education. How America's commitment to equity will determine our future.* New York, NY: Teachers College Press.

Delaney, K., & Neuman, S. B. (2018). Selling pre-K: Media, politics, and policy in the case of universal prekindergarten in New York City. *Teachers College Record 120*(4), 1–32.

Delaney, K., Whyte, K., & Graue, M. E. (2020). A vision of early childhood curriculum built on strong foundations. In J. J. Mueller & N. File (Eds.), *Curriculum in early childhood education: Re-examined, reclaimed, renewed* (pp. 193–208). New York, NY: Routledge.

Delgado, R., & Stefancic, J. (2001). *Critical race theory: An introduction.* New York, NY: New York University Press.

Derrida, J. (1978). *Writing and difference.* Chicago, IL: The University of Chicago Press.

Diffey, L. (2017). *50-state comparison: State kindergarten-through-third-grade policies.* Denver, CO: Education Commission of the States. Retrieved from www.ecs.org/wp-content/uploads/Age_Requirements_for_Free_and_Compulsory_Education-1.pdf

Dodge, D., Colker, L., & Heroman, C. (2002). *Creative curriculum for preschool* (4th ed.). Washington, DC: Teaching Strategies.

Douglass, A. (2017). *Leading for change in early care and education: Cultivating leadership from within.* New York, NY: Teachers College Press.

Early Childhood Collaborative & Arborville School District. (2003). *Early learning standards: Ages 3–5.* Flomot, TX: ASD Publisher.

EdBuild. (2019). *Nonwhite school districts get $23 billion less than white districts despite serving the same number of students.* Retrieved from edbuild.org/content/23-billion#CA

Emerson, R. M., Fretz, R. I., & Shaw L. L. (1995). *Writing ethnographic fieldnotes.* Chicago, IL: University of Chicago Press.

Ewen, D., Blank, H., Hart, K., & Schulman, K. (2001). *State developments in childcare, early education, and school-age care*. Washington, DC: Children's Defense Fund.

Fontana, A., & Frey, J. H. (1998). Interviewing: The art of science. In N. Denzin & Y. Lincoln (Eds.), *Collecting and interpreting qualitative materials*, (pp. 47–78) Thousand Oaks, CA: Sage.

Foucault, M. (1972). *The archaeology of knowledge*. London, UK: Irvington & Tavistock.

Foucault, M. (1980). *Power/knowledge: Selected interviews and other writings by Michel Foucault, 1972–1977* (C. Gordon, Trans. & Ed.). New York, NY: Pantheon Books.

Foucault, M. (1995). *Discipline and punish: The birth of the prison* (A. Sheridan, Trans.). New York, NY: Vintage Books.

Franklin, B. M., Bloch, M. N., & Popkewitz, T. (Eds.). (2003). *Educational partnerships and the state: The paradoxes of government, schools, children and families*. New York, NY: Palgrave Macmillan.

Frede, E. C. (1995). The role of program quality in producing early childhood program benefits. *The Future of Children, 5*(3), 115–132.

Friedman-Krauss, A., Barnett, W. S., Garver, K. A., Hodges, K. S., Weisenfeld, G. G., & DiCrecchio, N. (2019). *The state of preschool 2018*. New Brunswick, NJ: National Institute for Early Education Research.

Friedman-Krauss, A., Barnett, W. S., Weisenfeld, G. G., Kasmin, R., DiCrecchio, N., & Horowitz, M. (2018). *The state of preschool 2017*. New Brunswick, NJ: National Institute for Early Education Research.

Frost, J. L., Wortham, S. C., & Reifel, S. C. (2012). *Play and child development* (4th ed.). Upper Saddle River, NJ: Pearson.

Fuller, B. (2007). *Standardized childhood: The political and cultural struggle over early education*. Redwood City, CA: Stanford University Press.

Fuller, B. (2014). Preschool is important but it's more important for poor children. *Washington Post*. Retrieved from www.washingtonpost.com/opinions/preschool-is-important-but-its-more-important-for-poor-children/2014/02/09/79ff4ab4-8e96-11e3-b227-12a45d109e03_story.html?utm_term=.cac198d114c8

Gallagher, J., Clayton, J., & Heinemeir, S. (2001). *Study of education for four-year-olds: State initiatives*. Chapel Hill, NC: National Center for Early Development and Learning.

Gary, P. (2010, January). The decline of play and rise in children's mental disorders: There's a reason kids are more anxious and depressed than ever. *Psychology Today*. Retrieved from www.psychologytoday.com

Geiger, A. W., Livingstone, G., & Bialek, K. (2019, May 8). 6 facts about U.S. moms. Retrieved from www.pewresearch.org/fact-tank/2019/05/08/facts-about-u-s-mothers/

Gilliam, W., & Zigler, E. (2000). A critical meta-analysis of all evaluations of state-funded preschool from 1977–1998: Implications for policy, service delivery and program evaluation. *Early Childhood Research Quarterly, 15*(4), 441–473.

Gittell, J. H. (2008). Relationships and resilience: Care provider responses to pressures from managed care. *The Journal of Applied Behavioral Science, 44*(1), 25–47. doi:1-.1177/0021886307311469

Gittell, J. H., & Douglass, A. (2012). Relational bureaucracy: Structuring reciprocal relationships into roles. *Academy of Management Review, 37*(4), 709–733. doi:10.5465/amr.2010.0438

Gladwell, M. (2017). Miss Buchanan's period of adjustment [Season 2, Episode 3]. In *Revisionist history*. Retrieved from revisionisthistory.com/episodes/13-miss-buchanans-period-of-adjustment

Goble, C., & Horm, D. M. (2009). Infant–toddler services through community collaboration: Oklahoma's early childhood initiatives. *Zero to Three, 29*(6), 18–22.

Goffin, S. G. (2015). *Professionalizing early childhood education as a field of practice: A guide to the next era.* Saint Paul, MN: Redleaf Press.

Goldstein, L. S. (2007). Beyond the DAP versus standard dilemma: Examining the unforgiving complexity of kindergarten teaching in the United States. *Early Childhood Research Quarterly, 22*, 39–54.

Golinkoff, R., Hassinger-Das, B., & Hirsh-Pasek, K. (2017). The case of brain science and guided play: A developing story. *Young Children, 72*(2), Retrieved from www.naeyc.org/resources/pubs/yc/may2017/case-brain-science-guided-play

Gomez-Velez, N. (2015). Can universal pre-K overcome extreme race and income segregation to reach New York's neediest children? The importance of legal infrastructure and the limits of the law. *Cleveland State Law Review, 63*(2), 319–354.

González, N., Moll, L. C., & Amanti, C. (2005). *Funds of knowledge: Theorizing practice in households, communities, and classrooms.* Mahwah, NJ: Erlbaum.

Good, A. (2018). *Teachers at the table: Voice, agency, and advocacy in educational policymaking.* Lanham, MD: Lexington Books, Rowman & Littlefield.

Gormley, W. T., Phillips, D., & Gayer, T. (2008). Preschool programs can boost school readiness. *Science, 27*(320), 1723–1724.

Graf, E., Hernandez, M. W., & Bingham, R. S. (2016). *Preschool predictors of academic achievement in five kindergarten readiness domains: Oral language and literacy, math, science, social-emotional development and approaches to learning.* Chicago, IL: NORC. Retrieved from krfoundation.org/krf/site-content/uploads/2017/05/Kindergarten-Readiness-Predictors-Final-Report-120916.pdf

Graue, M. E. (2006). The answer is readiness, now what is the question? *Early Education & Development, 17*(1), 43–56.

Graue, M. E., Ryan, S., Wilinski, B., Northey, K., & Nocera, A. (2018). What guides pre-K programs? *Teachers College Record.120*(8), 1–36.

Graue, M. E., & Walsh, D. J. (1998). *Studying children in context.* Thousand Oaks, CA: Sage.

Graue, M. E., Whyte, K., & Delaney, K. K. (2014). Fostering culturally and developmentally responsive teaching through improvisational practice. *Journal of Early Childhood Teacher Education, 35*(4), 37–41. doi.org/10.1080/10901027.2014.968296

Grieshaber, S., & Cannella, G. S. (Eds.) (2001). *Embracing identities in early childhood education: Diversity and possibilities.* New York, NY: Teachers College Press.

Guggenheim, D. (Director). (2011). *Waiting for Superman* [DVD]. United States: Paramount Home Entertainment.

Hall, S., & Gieben, B. (1992). *Formations of modernity.* Cambridge, UK: Polity Press.

Hallinger, P., & Heck, R. H. (2010). Collaborative leadership and school improvement: Understanding the impact on school capacity and student learning. *School Leadership and Management, 30*(2), 95–110.

Haney-Lopez, I. (1997). *White by law: The legal construction of race.* New York, NY: New York University Press.

Hatch, J. A. (2002a). Accountability shovedown: Resisting the standards movement in early childhood education. *Phi Delta Kappan, 83*(6), 457–462.

Hatch, J. A. (2002b). *Doing qualitative research in education settings.* New York, NY: State University of New York Press.

Head Start Early Childhood Learning and Knowledge Center. (2009). *Head Start approach to school readiness—Overview.* Retrieved from eclkc.ohs.acf.hhs.gov/school-readiness/article/head-start-approach-school-readiness-overview

Heckman, J. J., Moon, S. H., Pinto, R., Savelyev, P. A., & Yavitz, A. (2010). The rate of return to the High/Scope Perry preschool program. *Journal of Public Economics, 94*(1–2), 114–128.

Heimer, L. G., & Klefstad, E. (2015). It's not really a menu because we can't pick what we want to do: Content integration in kindergarten contexts. *Global Studies of Childhood*, pp. 1–16. doi:10.1177/2043610615597133

Heimer, L. G, & Winokur, J. (2015). Preparing teachers of young children: How an interdisciplinary curriculum approach is understood, supported, and enacted among students and faculty. *Journal of Early Childhood Teacher Education, 36*(4). 289-308.

Helm, J. H., & Katz, L. (2016). *Young investigators. The project approach in the early years.* New York, NY: Teachers College Press.

Hodder, I. (1998). The interpretation of documents and material culture. In N. Denzin & Y. Lincoln (Eds.), *Collecting and interpreting qualitative materials* (pp. 110–129). London, UK: Sage.

Honig, M. (2003). Building policy from practice: District central office administrator's roles and capacity for implementing collaborative education policy. *Educational Administration Quarterly, 39*(3) 292–338.

Institute of Medicine. (2000). *From neurons to neighborhoods: The science of early childhood development.* Washington, DC: National Academies Press. doi.org/10.17226/9824

Institute of Medicine & National Research Council. (2015). *Transforming the workforce for children birth through age 8.* Washington, DC: National Academies Press.

Interlandi, J. (2018, January 9). Why are our most important teachers paid the least? *The New York Times Magazine.* Retrieved from nyti.ms/2EmzucP

Kaestle, C. (1983). *Pillars of the republic: Common schools and American society, 1780–1860.* New York, NY: Hill and Wang.

Kagan, S. L. (Ed.) (2019). *The early advantage: Building systems that work for young children.* New York, NY: Teachers College Press.

Kagan, S. L., & Gomez, R. (2015). *Early childhood governance: Choices and early learning.* New York, NY: Teachers College Press.

Karoly, L. A. (2012). Toward standardization of benefit-cost analyses of early childhood interventions. *Journal of Benefit-Cost Analysis, 3*(1), 1–43.

Kirp, D. (2007). *The sandbox investment: The preschool movement and kids-first politics.* Cambridge, MA: Harvard University Press.

Koball, H., & Jiang, Y. (2018). *Basic facts about low-income children: Children under 18 years, 2016.* New York, NY: National Center for Children in Poverty, Columbia University Mailman School of Public Health. Retrieved from www.nccp.org/publications/pub_1194.html

Ladson-Billings, G. J. (2004). Landing on the wrong note: The price we paid for *Brown. Educational Researcher, 33*(7), 3–13.

Ladson-Billings, G. J. (2006). *From the achievement gap to the education debt: Understanding achievement in U.S. schools.* Educational Researcher, *35*(7), 3–12.

Lather, P. (1991). *Getting smart.* New York, NY: Routledge.

Lipsey, M. W., Hofer, K. G., Dong, N., Farran, D. C., & Bilbrey, C. (2013). *Evaluation of the Tennessee voluntary prekindergarten program: Kindergarten and first grade follow-up results from the randomized control design* (Research report). Nashville, TN: Vanderbilt University, Peabody Research Institute.

Lockwood, A. T. (1996). Community collaboration and social capital: An interview with Gary G. Wehlage. *New Leaders for Tomorrow's Schools, 2*(1), 20–33. Retrieved from files.eric.ed.gov/fulltext/ED426479.pdf

Lubeck, S. (2001). Early childhood education and care: A cross-national perspective. *Phi Delta Kappan, 83*(3), 213–215.

Lundkvist, M., Nyby, J., Autto, J., & Nygard, M. (2017). From universalism to selectivity? The background, discourses and ideas of recent early childhood education and care reforms in Finland. *Early Child Development and Care, 187*(10), 1543–1556.

Martin, L. H., Gutman, H., & Hutton, P. H. (Eds.). (1988). *Technologies of the self: A seminar with Michel Foucault.* Amherst, MA: University of Massachusetts Press.

Masterson, M. L., & Bohart, H. (Eds.). (2019). *Serious fun: How guided play extends children's learning.* Washington, DC: National Association for the Education of Young Children.

Mayall, B. (2002). *Towards a sociology of childhood: Thinking from children's lives.* Maidenhead, UK: Open University Press.

McCoy, D. C., Yoshikawa, H., Ziol-Guest, K. M., Duncan, G. J., Schindler, H. S., Magnuson, K., & Shonkoff, J. P. (2017). Impacts of early childhood education on medium- and long-term educational outcomes. *Educational Researcher, 46*(8), 474–487. doi.org/10.3102/0013189X17737739

McLean, C., Dichter, H., & Whitebook, M. (2017). *Strategies in pursuit of pre-K teacher compensation parity: Lessons from seven states and cities.* Berkeley, CA: Center for the Study of Child Care Employment, University of California, Berkeley, & New Brunswick, NJ: National Institute for Early Education Research.

Meatto, K. (2019, May 2). Still separate, still unequal: Teaching about school segregation and educational inequality. *New York Times.* Retrieved from www.nytimes.com/2019/05/02/learning/lesson-plans/still-separate-still-unequal-teaching-about-school-segregation-and-educational-inequality.html

Mervosh, S. (2019, February 27). How much wealthier are white school districts than nonwhite ones? $23 billion, report says. *New York Times.* Retrieved from www.nytimes.com/2019/02/27/education/school-districts-funding-white-minorities.html?module=inline

Michael-Luna, S., Grey, L., Brown, C. P., Peters, L., Castner, D., & Heimer, L. (2019). *From policy to practice: Exploring the "implementation gap" in early childhood education.* AERA panel presentation, Toronto, Ontario, Canada.

Michael-Luna, S., Heimer, L., & Grey, L. (2020). Unpacking the tensions in open-ended preschool curriculum: Teacher agency, standardization, and English learners in creative curriculum and high/scope. In J. J. Mueller & N. File (Eds.), *Curriculum in early childhood education: Re-examined, reclaimed, renewed* (pp. 114–128). New York, NY: Routledge.

Michel, S. (1999). *Children's interests/mother's rights: The shaping of America's child care policy.* New Haven, CT: Yale University Press.

Michel, S. (2011). *The history of child care in the U.S.* Social Welfare History Project, Virginia Commonwealth University. Retrieved from socialwelfare.library.vcu.edu/programs/child-care-the-american-history/

Minervino, J. (2014). *Lessons from research and the classroom: Implementing high-quality pre-K that makes a difference for young children.* Seattle, WA: Bill and Melinda Gates Foundation.

Mueller, J. J. & File, N. (Eds.), (2020). *Curriculum in early childhood education: Re-examined, reclaimed, renewed.* New York, NY: Routledge.

National Association for the Education of Young Children (NAEYC). (2009). *Developmentally appropriate practice in early childhood programs serving children from birth to age 8* [Position statement]. Retrieved from www.naeyc.org/sites/default/s/globally-shared/downloads/PDFs/resources/position-statements/PSDAP.pdf

National Association for the Education of Young Children (NAEYC). (2016, May 25). *New national collaboration to set professional guidelines for all early childhood* [Press release]. Retrieved from www.naeyc.org/our-work/initiatives/profession/naeyc-announces-new-national-collaboration

National Education Association (NEA). (2019). *Early childhood education.* Retrieved from www.nea.org/home/18210.htm

National Governors Association Center for Best Practices & Council of Chief State School Officers. (2010). *Common Core State Standards.* Washington, DC: Author.

Nell, M. L., Drew, W. F., & Bush D. E. (2013). *From play to practice: Connecting teachers' play to children's learning.* Washington, DC: National Association for the Education of Young Children.

Nelson, K. (2009). *Young minds in social worlds: Experience, meaning, and memory.* Cambridge, MA: Harvard University Press.

New Zealand Ministry of Education. (2018, March 21). Retrieved from www.education.govt.nz/early-childhood/teaching-and-learning/te-whariki/

Palmer, P. (1994). Leading from within: Out of the shadows and into the light. In J. Conger (Ed.), *Spirit at work* (pp. 19–40). San Francisco, CA: Jossey-Bass.

Palmer, P. (2017). *The courage to teach: Exploring the inner landscape of a teacher's life.* San Francisco, CA: Jossey-Bass.

Parker, E., Diffey, L., & Atchison, B. (2018). *How states fund pre-K: A primer for policymakers.* Retrieved from www.ecs.org/wp-content/uploads/How-States-Fund-Pre-K_A-Primer-for-Policymakers.pdf

Parker, E., Keily, T., Atchison, B., & Mullen, J. (2019). *Trends in pre-K education funding in 2017-18* (Policy brief). Education Commission of the States.

Peshkin, A. (1988). In search of subjectivity—one's own. *Educational Researcher, 17*(7), 17–21.

Petersen, E. (2003). *Early childhood curriculum.* Boston, MA: Allyn & Bacon.

Pinar, W. (2004). *What is curriculum theory?* Mahwah, NJ: Erlbaum.

Popkewitz, T. S. (1998). *Struggling for the soul.* New York, NY: Teachers College Press.

Rabinow, P. (Ed.). (1984). *The Foucault reader.* New York, NY: Pantheon Books.

Ravitch, D. (2016). *The death and life of the great American school system: How testing and choice are undermining education.* New York, NY: Basic Books.

Resnick, M. (2011). Pre-K programs are a long-term investment worth making. *American School Board Journal, 198*(5), 6–7.

Reynolds, A. J., Temple, J. A, Robertson, D. L., & Mann, E. A. (2001). *Long-term effects of an early childhood intervention on educational achievement and juvenile arrest: A 15-year follow-up of low-income children in public schools.* Retrieved from www.waisman.wisc.edu/cls/cbaexecsum4.html

Reynolds, A. J., Wang, M. C., & Walberg, H. J. (Eds.). (2003). *Early childhood programs for a new century.* Washington, DC: CWLA Press.

Riley, D., San Juan, R. R., Klinkner, J., Ramminger, A., with Carns, M., Burns, M., . . . Clark-Ericksen, C. (2007). *Social and emotional development: Connecting science and practice in early childhood settings.* Saint Paul, MN: Redleaf Press.

Rist, R. (1998). Influencing the policy process with qualitative research. In N. Denzin & Y. Lincoln (Eds.), *Collecting and interpreting qualitative materials* (pp. 400–424). London, UK: Sage.

Rodd, J. (2012). *Leadership in early childhood*. Maidenhead, UK: Open University Press.

Rogoff, B. (2003). *The cultural nature of human development*. New York, NY: Oxford University Press.

Roosevelt, E. (1944, August). *Woman's place after the war*. Virginia Commonwealth University Libraries Social Welfare History Project. Retrieved from socialwelfare. library.vcu.edu/woman-suffrage/womans-place-war/

Ryan, C. (2001). Leadership in collaborative policy-making: An analysis of agency roles in regulatory negotiations. *Policy Sciences, 34*, 221–245.

Ryan, S., & Grieshaber, S. (2004). It's more than child development: Critical theories, research, and teaching young children. *Young Children, 5*(6), 44–52.

Sachs, J. (2000). Inequities in early care and education: What is America buying? *Journal of Education for Students Placed at Risk, 5*(4), 383–395.

Sandfort, J., & Selden, S. C. (2001). Blurring the boundaries: Local collaborations among Head Start, preschool and child care programs. *Policy & Practice of Public Human Services, 59*(1), 18–23.

Schulman, K., & Blank, H. (2009). *Building community collaboration to support early learning: Local councils for early care and education*. Washington, DC: National Women's Law Center.

Schumacher, R., Hamm, K., & Ewen, D. (2007). *Making pre-kindergarten work for low-income working families*. Center for Law and Social Policy Child and Early Education Policy (1). Retrieved from www.clasp.org/publications/report/brief/ making-pre-kindergarten-work-low-income-working-families

Schweinhart, L. J., & Weikart, D. (1997). High/Scope Educational Research Foundation. *Early Childhood Research Quarterly, 12*, 117–143.

Scott, L. C. (2005). Leadership matters: Governors' pre-k proposals fiscal year 2006. Retrieved from www.preknow.org/documents/LeadershipReport.pdf

Seddon, T., Billett, S., & Clemans, A. (2004). Politics of social partnerships: A framework for theorizing. *Journal of Education Policy, 19*(2), 123–142. doi:10.1080/014434104 2000186309

Seddon, T., Billett, S., & Clemans, A. (2005). Navigating social partnerships: Central agencies—local networks. *British Journal of Sociology of Education, 26*(5), 567–584.

Seefeldt, C., & Wasik, B. A. (2006). *Early education: Three-, four-, and five-year-olds go to school*. Upper Saddle River, NJ: Pearson/Merrill/Prentice Hall.

Selden, S. C., Sowa, J. E., & Sandfort, J. R. (2006). The impact of nonprofit collaboration in early childcare and education on management and program outcomes. *Public Administration Review, 66*(3), 412–425. doi.org/10.1111/j.1540-6210.2006.00598.x

Semega, J., Fontenot, K. R., & Kollar, M. A. (2017). *Income and poverty in the United States: 2016*. Retrieved from www.census.gov/library/publications/2017/demo/p60-259.html

Senge, P. (1990). *The fifth discipline*. New York, NY: Doubleday.

Sensoy, O., & DiAngelo, R. J. (2017). *Is everyone really equal? An introduction to key concepts in social justice education*. New York, NY: Teachers College Press.

Shaefer, L., Duncan, G. J., Edin, K., Garfinkel, I., Harris, D., Smeeding, T., . . . Yoshikawa, H. (2018). A universal child allowance: A plan to reduce poverty and income instability among children in the United States. *RSF: Russell Sage Foundation Journal of the Social Sciences, 4*(2), 22–42.

Shonkoff, J. P., & Philllps, D. A. (Eds.). (2000). *From neurons to neighborhoods: The science of early childhood development*. Washington, DC: National Academies Press.

Silin, J. G., & Lippman, C. (2003). *Putting the children first: The changing face of Newark's public schools*. New York, NY: Teachers College Press.

Siskel Jacobs Productions. (2018). *No small matter. High quality education for all isn't just powerful—it's possible*. Retrieved from www.nosmallmatter.com/

Smith, S. (2015). *Against race- and class-based pedagogy in early childhood education*. New York, NY: Palgrave Macmillan.

Spencer, T. (2014). Preschool for all? Examining the current policy context in light of Genishi's research. *Contemporary Issues in Early Childhood, 15*(2), 176–184.

Spillane, J. P., Halverson, R., & Diamond, J. B. (2001). Investigating school leadership practice: A distributed perspective. *Educational Researcher, 30*(3), 23–28.

Spradley, J. P. (1980). *Participant observation*. New York, NY: Holt, Rinehart, and Winston.

Stake, R. E. (1995). *The art of case study research*. Thousand Oaks, CA: Sage.

Strauss, D. (2002). *How to make collaboration work*. San Francisco, CA: Berrett-Koehler.

Sykes, M. (2014). *Doing the right thing for children: Eight qualities of leadership*. St. Paul, MN: Redleaf Press.

Thompson, R. A. (2014). Stress and child development. *The Future of Children, 24*(1), 41–59.

Underwood, P. (1993). *The walking people: A Native American oral history*. Austin, TX: Tribe of Two Press.

U.S. Department of Health and Human Services (2003). State funded pre-kindergarten: What the evidence shows. Retrieved from aspe.hhs.gov/hsp/state-funded-pre-k/index.htm

U.S. Department of Labor. (2019). Family and Medical Leave Act. Retrieved from www.dol.gov/whd/fmla/

United States Government Accountability Office. (2004). *Prekindergarten: Four selected states expanded access by relying on schools and existing providers of early education and care to provide services*. Retrieved from www.gao.gov/cgi-bin/getrpt?GAO-04-852.

Warren, E. (2019). Warren unveils universal child care and early learning proposal. Retrieved from www.warren.senate.gov/newsroom/press-releases/warren-unveils-universal-child-care-and-early-learning-proposal

Weiland, C., & Yoshikawa, H. (2013). Impacts of a prekindergarten program on children's mathematics, language, literacy, executive function, and emotional skills. *Child Development, 84*(6), 2112–2130.

Weisberg, D. S., Kittredge, A. K., Hirsh-Pasek, K., Golinkoff, R. M., & Klahr, D. (2015). Making play work for education. *Phi Delta Kappan, 96*(8), 8–13.

Wells, K. (2015). *Childhood in global perspective*. Cambridge, UK: Polity Press.

Wenger, E. (1998). *Communities of practice: Learning, meaning, and identity*. Cambridge, UK: Cambridge University Press.

Wheatley, M. J. (1992). *Leadership and the new science: Learning about organizations from an orderly universe*. San Francisco, CA: Berrett-Koehler.

Whitebook, M., & Ryan, S. (2012). More than teachers: The Early Care and Education Workforce. In R. C. Pianta, W. S. Barnett, L. M. Justice, & S. M. Sheridan (Eds.), *Handbook of early childhood education* (pp. 92–110). New York, NY: Guilford Press.

Whitehurst, G. J. (2014). Does pre-k work? It depends how picky you are. *The Brookings Institution*. Retrieved from www.brookings.edu/research/does-pre-k-work-it-depends-how-picky-you-are/

Whyte, K., & Karabon, A. (2016). Transforming teacher–family relationships: Shifting roles and perceptions of home visits through the funds of knowledge approach. *Early Years, 36*(2), 207–221.

Wilinski, B. (2017a). Plays well with others: The discourse and enactment of partnerships in public pre-K. In J. Lester, C. Lochmiller, & R. Gabriel (Eds.), *Discursive perspectives on education policy and implementation* (pp. 133–156). New York, NY: Palgrave Macmillan.

Wilinski, B. (2017b). *Pre-K comes to school.* New York, NY: Teachers College Press.

Wisneski, D. B., & Reifel, S. (2012). The place of play in early childhood curriculum. In N. File, J. J. Mueller, & D. B. Wisnewski (Eds.), *Curriculum in early childhood education: Re-examined, rediscovered, renewed* (175–187). New York, NY: Routledge.

Wohlwend, K., & Peppler, K. (2015). All rigor and no play is no way to improve learning. *Phi Delta Kappan, 96*(8), 22–26.

Wollons, R. (2000). *Kindergartens and cultures.* New Haven, CT: Yale University Press.

Wong, V. C., Cook, T. D., Barnett, W. S., & Jung, K. (2008). An effectiveness-based evaluation of five state pre-kindergarten programs. *Journal of Policy Analysis and Management, 27*(1), 122–154.

Zigler, E., Gilliam W. S., & Barnett, W. S. (2011). *The pre-K debates: Current controversies and issues.* Baltimore, MD: Brookes.

Zigler, E., Gilliam, W. S., & Jones, S. M. (2006). *A vision for universal preschool education.* New York, NY: Cambridge University Press.

Index

About the Authors

Lucinda G. Heimer, PhD, associate professor and program coordinator of the Early Childhood/Special Education dual licensure program at the University of Wisconsin–Whitewater, has taught future educators for over 15 years. Dr. Heimer has published on topics including interdisciplinary curriculum, collaboration, and race in peer-reviewed journals, as well as authored chapters in multiple edited texts. She has presented her research using critical theory and duoethnography to illuminate practicing and future teacher perspectives regarding identity, race, and social justice in early education, specifically working with Indigenous communities. Creating pathways for future teachers to earn credentials to teach in their home communities is at the heart of this work. Having received recognition for her teaching at the college level, she is most grateful to the students at both undergraduate and graduate levels. She has supervised students in urban, rural, and suburban school districts in birth through 3rd-grade settings. Her experience includes teaching preschool and elementary school children and directing university lab and parent cooperative preschools. Her appreciation for the complexity of collaboration and issues of equity run deep.

Ann Elizabeth Ramminger, MS, founder of Early Childhood Solutions Consulting, understands the complexity of cross-system efforts and collaboration, based on her experience in a variety of early childhood systems, including Head Start, public schools, special education, public health, home visiting, child care, mental health, universities, and state early childhood systems. Ms. Ramminger has been involved in developing early learning standards, core competencies, and other efforts to strengthen the early childhood system. She has co-authored three books about child development focusing on nutrition, cognition, and social–emotional development. She is passionate about connecting and presenting research and practice for the early childhood profession, related professionals, and the public, in practical, user-friendly, and accessible ways.

Contributing Authors:

Katherine K. Delaney, PhD, assistant professor, Early Childhood and Special Education, Judith Herb College of Education, University of Toledo, Ohio

Katherine K. Delaney is an assistant professor of Early Childhood Education at the University of Toledo. Kate's research focuses on how teachers, children, and families experience the impacts of federal, state, and/or local policies in their daily lives in early childhood settings. Her recent work has been focused on Head Start and Title 1 preschool classrooms in Ohio. Formerly, Kate was a preschool teacher in New York City and Milwaukee, Wisconsin.

Sarah Galanter-Guziewski, *principal, Stephens Elementary School, Madison Metropolitan School District, Madison, Wisconsin*
Sarah Galanter-Guziewski has been the principal at Glenn Stephens elementary school in Madison, Wisconsin for 12 years. Her previous work included: K/1 bilingual and 4K classroom teacher, Education Peace Corps volunteer in Paraguay, and after-school coordinator at the East Harlem Tutorial Program. Sarah has a bachelor's from Tufts in child development, a master's in social service administration from the University of Chicago, and a master's in educational leadership from Cardinal Stritch.

Lacey Peters, *PhD, assistant professor, Early Childhood Education, Department of Curriculum and Teaching, Hunter College of the City University of New York*
Lacey Peters is an assistant professor of early childhood education at Hunter College of the City University of New York. Her research interests are broad, and she examines the viewpoints and decisionmaking processes of children, parents and other family members, and early childhood professionals. She is currently working on a project that foregrounds Universal Prekindergarten teachers' perspectives on using authentic assessment systems.

Kristin Whyte, *PhD, assistant professor, Mount Mary University, Milwaukee, Wisconsin*
Kristin Whyte is an assistant professor at Mount Mary University. She began her career as an early childhood and public elementary school teacher. She received her PhD from the University of Wisconsin, Madison in curriculum and instruction and completed postgraduate work at Northwestern University conducting educational policy research. Kristin's work focuses on early childhood teaching and learning, relationships between home and school, educational policies' impacts on schools, and the construction of socially just educational practices.